VOLUME 12

Silver Spoon

HIROMU ARAKAWA

STORY & CHARACTERS

ICHIROU KOMABA

A former student at Ooezo Agricultural High School, enrolled in the Dairy Science Program. He had planned on taking over the family farm after graduation, but it went out of business.

AKI MIKAGE

A student at Ooezo Agricultural High School, enrolled in the Dairy Science Program. While her family has accepted that their only daughter won't carry on the family business, now she has to get into college...

YUUGO HACHIKEN

A student at Ooezo Agricultural High School, enrolled in the Dairy Science Program. A city kid from Sapporo who got in through the general entrance exam. He found a goal—starting a business—but it's proving to be tricky...

AYAME MINAMIKUJOU

Aki's childhood friend. Started an Equestrian Club at Shimizu West High School to compete with her. Sees Hachiken as a rival too, for some reason.

TAMAKO INADA

A student at Ooezo Agricultural High School, enrolled in the Dairy Science Program. Her family runs a megafarm. She's helping Hachiken start his business.

The Story Thus Far:

Hachiken has finally set a goal: starting a business. He's outlined his business plan and asked Tamako to check it over multiple times, but even with their combined efforts, it hasn't been approved. It seems they still need more to convince his father to invest in his business idea... Meanwhile, Hachiken's fruitless boarding house search is safely settled with the help of the Mikage family, once again driving home for him just how important it is to have connections with others. Hachiken moves out of the dorm he called home for the span of an entire year, and on the first day of his new boarder life, Ookawa-senpai drops by with a gas burner in hand—only for it to explode in Hachiken's room. It's still only move-in day, and Hachiken already has a disaster on his hands...

SHINEI OOKAWA

A graduate of Ooezo Agricultural High School's Agricultural Engineering Program and former Equestrian Club president. He graduated without finding permanent employment, so now he's unemployed...

CONTENTS

Chapter 97
Tale of Winter ㉞

PEOPLE WITH NO BRAND ALL COMING TOGETHER TO INCREASE THEIR INCOMES, HUH...?
SO SOMETHING LIKE, YOU KNOW, THE INADAS' FARM?
SMALL FARMS COMBINING INTO ONE GIANT BUSINESS? A JOINT-MANAGEMENT SYSTEM?
HACHI, YOU GOT ANY BIG PLOTS OF FARMLAND?
YOU KNOW I DON'T!
SO WHAT'RE YOU GONNA DO WITH ZERO CAPITAL?
LIKE I SAID, I HAVE TO GET MONEY FROM MY PARENTS FIRST...
STICKER: ASURA II
NON-FARMERS CAN'T GET THEIR HANDS ON FARMLAND THAT EASILY.
NOPE, THERE IS ONE EASY SHORTCUT.
MARRY INTO THE MIKAGE FAMILY.

THEY GOT NOBODY TO CARRY ON THE FAMILY BUSINESS, RIGHT? YOU JUMP IN, AND IT'S AS GOOD AS YOURS.
AS THE SON-IN-LAW SUCCESSOR OF FARMERS, YOU COULD GETCHER HANDS ON PLENTY OF LAND WITHOUT JUMPIN' THROUGH ANY HOOPS.
OH, THERE'D BE HOOPS!! LIKE HOW ABOUT HOW MIKAGE FEELS!!?
WHY DO YOU GUYS KEEP TRYING TO DESTROY THE TRUST I'VE BUILT UP SLOW AND STEADY?!
THERE'S REALLY NOTHIN' GOIN' ON BETWEEN YOU TWO? YOU AIN'T DATIN'?
I'VE TOLD YOU, IF ANYTHING GOES ON BEFORE MIKAGE GETS INTO COLLEGE, HER DAD WILL MURDER ME!!
WIMP!!
OTHER'S FEELINGS?
IF YOU WANT TO GO INTO BUSINESS WITH NO MONEY, LAND, OR GOODS TO YOUR NAME, THEN CUT THE NICE GUY CRAP.
KEH! PTOO!
H...HAVING NOTHING MEANS I CAN BECOME ANYTHING! MY FUTURE SPARKLES WITH POSSIBILITY! AIKAWA SAID SO!!
IF YOU'RE GOING FOR LARGE-SCALE INTENSIVE FARMING WITH JOINT MANAGEMENT, WHY DON'TCHA JUST MODEL IT AFTER TAMAKO'S FARM?
I DUNNO...A SYSTEM THAT STANDARDIZED DOESN'T QUITE FIT WHAT I'M GOING FOR...
I WANT THE PARTICIPANTS TO BE ABLE TO GROUP UP WHILE STILL KEEPING THEIR INDIVIDUAL QUIRKS...
UHHH...LIKE, FOR EVERYONE TO STAND AS EQUALS WITHIN THE GROUP, WHETHER THEIR FARM IS AS PERSONAL AS KOMABA'S OR AS BUSINESS-LIKE AS TAMAKO'S, WITHOUT BEING REJECTED...

SOUNDS LIKE THIS COULD BE A LONG CONVERSATION.
GO BUY US SOME SUPPER, HACHIKEN.
AH, SURE THING.
THANK YOUUU.
...WAIT, HUH?
WHY AM I THE GOFER?
...HE WENT OFF TO GO FETCH LIKE IT WAS ONLY NATURAL.
HE SEEMS LIKE A FAILURE AT FIRST GLANCE, BUT THIS IS WHERE HACHIKEN REALLY SHINES.
GUYS WHO GO TO GREAT LENGTHS FOR OTHERS? PEOPLE WILL FOLLOW 'EM TO THE END OF THE WORLD.
YOU SAID IT. HE'S WORLDS APART FROM YOU, OOKAWA-SENPAI.

Spring Break Stable Duty
4/1 Yoda, Maruyama
2 Hachiken, Maruyama
3 Hachiken, Mikage
4 Kino, Mikage
5 Kino, Sakae
Yoda
I'll be gone starting on 4/2 for farm work at home.
THE YEAR 603.
THE TWELVE LEVEL CAP AND RANK SYSTEM.
THE YEAR 607.
THE MISSIONS TO SUI CHINA.
GET IT MOVED, GET IT MOVED...
THE YEAR 645.
THE TAIKA REFORM.
710?
THE CAPITAL RELOCATES TO NARA.
712?
THE KOJIKI RECORDS.
HUP-HO!
HUP-HO!
HUP-HO!
720?
THE NIHON SHOKI CHRONICLES.
743?
UMMM... THE KONDEN EINEN SHIZAI LAW ALLOWS FARMERS TO PERMANENTLY OWN PRIVATE LAND!
EASY DOES IT!

CHROME.
Cr.
TITANI-
UM.
Ti.
SILVER.
Ag.
MOLYB-
DENUM.
Mo.
ARF!
U
!
ARF?
WHO'S
THIS?
HELLO?
BIKU
(FLINCH)

...HI...
HERE TO SEE THE CLUB, YOU THINK?
MIGHT JUST BE LOST.
UH...
ERM...
I'M...
...AN EZO AG STUDENT STARTING THIS YEAR.
A NEW STU-DENT!
WOW.
I'M IN THE DAIRY SCIENCE PROGRAM.
THAT'S GREAT! CONGRAT-ULATIONS ON GETTING IN!
DAIRY SCIENCE, HUH? DOES YOUR FAMILY RUN A FARM?
N...NO, MY DAD IS...A CIVIL SERVANT!

OH, YOU'RE FROM A NON-FARMING FAMILY?
HEY, ME TOO.
OH ...!
SO YOU'RE GOING TO PURSUE A CAREER RELATED TO DAIRY FARMING, THEN?
UH... UM, UH, NO...
I WASN'T PICKY ABOUT THE PRO-GRAM...
ERM...
AT FIRST, I APPLIED FOR THE FOOD SCIENCE PROGRAM WITH A RECOMMENDATION... BUT IT WAS MORE COMPETITIVE THAN I EXPECTED, AND I DIDN'T GET IN...
EH?
DON'T TELL US...
YOU REAPPLIED FOR DAIRY SCIENCE THROUGH GENERAL ADMIS-SIONS!?
...Y-YEAH!
THERE WAS ONE SPOT OPEN, SO!
WHY GO THAT FAR TO GET IN?
....
....
....
....

...THE HORSES...
I... LIKED THEM...
AT EZO AG FEST I WATCHED THE SHOW JUMPING AND DRAFT HORSE RACES!!
ERM... I WAS SUPER-SHOOK!!
LIKE, IT LIT THIS FIRE IN MY HEART!!
I...DON'T KNOW THE FIRST THING ABOUT HORSES...
B...B-B-B-BUT AFTER THAT, I DECIDED TO JOIN EZO AG'S E-E-E-EQUESTRIAN CLUB...
AND I HAVE NOTHING TO DO SINCE IT'S SPRING BREAK, SO...
...I CAME TO CHECK IT OUT...

Campis
Guest Book
Feel free to share any thoughts and comments as well.
Equestrian Club
THANKS.
HUH?
...YOU'RE NOT GONNA LAUGH AT ME?
FOR WHAT?
I'M A TOTAL AMATEUR WHO ENROLLED AT A FARM SCHOOL FOR THE HORSES AFTER SEEING ONE LITTLE RACE...
GONYO GONYO (MUMBLE)
I'M SORRY. ERR...FOR BEING SUCH A SHEEP...

DID SOMEONE GIVE YOU A HARD TIME FOR IT?
YEAH... MY PARENTS AND STUFF...
THEY WERE ALL LIKE, "HORSES AND FARMING ARE HARD WORK! DO YOU EVEN KNOW WHAT YOU'RE GETTING INTO?"...
馬術部
PAINFULLY FAMILIAR
TH... THIS IS... TOTALLY THAT TYPE OF KID. SHE'S ME FROM NOT THAT LONG AGO.
THE TYPE WHO'S LOST ALL THEIR SELF-CONFIDENCE ...!!
ODO (FRET) おど
ODO おど
JACKET: OOEZO AGRICULTURAL HIGH SCHOOL EQUESTRIAN CLUB
DON'T WORRY ABOUT WHAT YOUR PARENTS SAY!
IT WAS LIKE THAT FOR ME TOO. YOU GET USED TO THE HARD WORK!!
ONCE YOU COLLAPSE FOR THE FIRST TIME, YOU LEARN YOUR LIMITS!!
AND BE-SIDES ...
...WE'RE ALL TOTAL AMATEURS IN THE BEGINNING.
WE WON'T LAUGH AT YOU.

AH!
YOU FINALLY LOOKED US IN THE EYES.
!
TAKE YOUR TIME CHECKING THINGS OUT.
O... OKAY!!
THANKS MUCHLY!!
BHRRN?
DOKI (BADUM)
DOKI
ドキドキドキ
DOKI
RE-TESTING AFTER SHE FAILED? I'M IMPRESEED.
YUP. SHE'S BRAVE.
...WHAT WOULD YOU DO, MIKAGE?
OSORU
おそるおそる
OSORU (TIMID)
HUH?

IF YOU FAIL YOUR RECOMMENDATION APPLICATION TO OOEZO UNIVERSITY OF ANIMAL HUSBANDRY...
DON'T JINX ME!!
I'D TRY AGAIN THROUGH THE GENERAL ADMISSIONS EXAM, OBVIOUSLY.
馬術部
SNORT!
馬術部
YEAH.
I KNEW YOU'D SAY THAT.
ぺちょ
PECHO (NUDGE)
EEP!
HEY!
IF IT'S TOO STINKY OR TOO SCARY, IT'S OKAY! YOU DON'T HAVE TO FORCE YOURSELF TO JOIN!
O-O-O... OKAY!!!
AH...NO, THAT'S NOT WHAT I MEANT!!
むっし
MUSSHI (GNAW)
むっし
MUSSHI
I'M JOINING!! LIKE, DEFINITE-LY!!
TH-TH-TH... THANKS FOR HAVING ME!!
SURE THING. THAT'S AWESOME.

WELCOME TO THE EZO AG EQUESTRIAN CLUB!
Ooezo Agricultural High School 2012
Entrance Ceremony

Project Presentations
Team Formation
AT EZO AG, ALL YOU HAVE TO DO IS SAY YOU WANT TO DO SOMETHING, AND THEY'LL LET YOU TRY JUST ABOUT ANYTHING.
WHETHER YOU'LL FAIL OR SUCCEED IS SOMETHING SEPARATE.
PROJECT: CREATE A NEW PORK BRAND
EVEN WHEN YOU SAY SOMETHING STRANGE, THE TEACHERS DON'T LAUGH. THEY'LL SAY, "GIVE IT A TRY."
ANIMAL WELFARE
THEY GIVE YOU A CHANCE.
Cheese Research Club Plus Whey-Fed Pigs ♡
Ezo Ag Sausage Club
EZO AG BACON CLUB

EZO AG BACON CLUB
Ezo Ag Sausage Club
Project Chickin Club
EVEN IF YOU FAIL, SOMEONE ELSE WILL PICK UP WHERE YOU LEFT OFF. THEY'LL FINISH THE PROJECT FOR YOU.
THEY'LL TURN WHAT YOU WANTED TO ACHIEVE INTO REALITY.
CLASS 2-A PROJECT
BRING IT ON! GLOBAL WARMING
EFFECTS OF AVERAGE TEMPERAT
INCREASE ON HOKKAIDO CROPS
100% EZO AG-MADE PIZZA PROJECT
AND THAT WILL TIE BACK INTO THE NEXT DREAM.
Large-Scal
Intensive Farm
Revamp an
International
SOMETIMES IT CAN BECOME A PAIN IN THE ASS THAT THEY DON'T LET YOU QUIT, BUT THERE WILL COME A DAY WHEN YOU KIND OF APPRECIATE IT.
THAT'S WHY I'M SHOOTING FOR A PROJECT ABOUT MAKING EVERYONE'S DREAMS COME TRUE BY ASKING EACH OTHER FOR HELP AND GIVING IT.

KAKYU (SQUEAK)
かきゅ
KAKYU
かきゅ
Farming Bonds
Business
SCHOOL PRECEPTS: WORK, COLLABORATE, DEFY LOGIC
校訓 勤労 協同 理不尽
Project Presentations
Team Formation
Farming Bonds Business
SOMEONE WHO DOESN'T REJECT OTHERS' DREAMS...
THAT'S WHO I WANT TO BE.

ギ…
GI (CREAK)
ガシャン
GASHAN (KCHAK)
WEL-COME HOME, DEAR.
YOU HAD A LONG DAY.
MM. GOOD TO BE HOME.
A PACKAGE CAME FROM YUUGO.
ズシ…
ZUSHI (HEFT)
EXPRESS HOME DELIVERY
Proposal
A CUP OF TEA...
... PLEASE.
どかっ
DOKA (FWUMP)
TEA?
YOU'RE STAY-ING UP?
YES.
YOU CAN GO TO BED WITHOUT ME.

THIS IS A TROUBLESOME AND IMPORTANT FAMILY MATTER.

I'LL HANDLE IT AT ONCE.

Chapter 97: Tale of Winter End

Silver Spoon

ALEXANDRA DOROHOVICH

SHINGO HACHIKEN'S WIFE
RUSSIAN
DESCENDED FROM UKRAINIAN
COSSACKS

OH? YOU GOT KOMABA'S CONTACT INFO?
YEAH, THROUGH MIKAGE.
MRRRGH...
MONEY MUST BE REALLY TIGHT FOR KOMABA'S FAMILY...
I GUESS I'D SAY HE'S GETTING MORE POSITIVE BIT BY BIT.
HE'S STARTED REPLYING TO RANDOM MESSAGES TOO...
can't get hired as a farmhand without a driver's license
still can't find a buyer for our land cuz it's so rough and by the mountains
BUT IT SOUNDS LIKE HIS FAMILY SITUATION IS STILL AS GRIM AS BEFORE...

Chapter 98
Tale of Four Seasons①

Chapter 98:
Tale of Four Seasons ①

HAKUYUUKAI TOKACHI HORSE RIDING MEET
HO HO HO HO HO!!
VAA (BWOOSH)
I'M SURE YOU'VE ALL MISSED ME, EZO AG!!

The Tale of Ayame Minamikujou

......
YOU'RE ALWAYS SO VIVACIOUS, AYAME-CHAN.
HEY, MINAMIKUJOU. DID YOU LEARN THE RULES?
HO HO HO HO HO!
RULES? WHAT NONSENSE! RULES CHANGE WITH THE TIMES!! WHAT'S THE POINT OF LEARNING THEM!?
HO HO HO HO HO HO HO!

WHAT'S THIS? ARE YOU AN EZO AG RECRUIT?
... YES!
SHE'S ALWAYS SO SERIOUSLY DUMB...
ONLY ONE?
WE HAD FIVE NEW KIDS AT FIRST...
...BUT FOUR OF THEM UP AND QUIT 'COS OF THE EARLY MORNINGS AND BACK-BREAKING WORK.
HO-HO-HO-HO-HO! THE EZO AG EQUESTRIAN CLUB IS TOO PATHETIC!!!
DO YOU TRULY THINK YOU'LL BE ABLE TO BEST SHIMIZU WEST HIGH, LED BY *MOI*, AYAME MINAMIKUJOU, WITH SUCH A SAD SHOWING!?
HOW MANY NEWBIES DID YOU GET?
I AM THE ONLY ONE AND THE NUMBER ONE!!!
SO YOU'RE ALL BY YOUR LONESOME.
The Tokachi Region Spring Horse Riding Meet will now begin.

DOGA (KA-CLOP)
PACHI
PACHI
PACHI
PACHI
PACHI (CLAP)
WHOOOA!
PACHI
PACHI
PACHI
PACHI
PACHI

The Tale of Shinei Ookawa

OOKAWA-SAN, GOOD TO SEE YOU.

I CAME TO SEE MY JUNIORS' HEROIC EXPLOITS WHILE TAKING MY LITTLE BUDDY HERE ON A WALK.

HUH? SENPAI, I DIDN'T KNOW YOU HAD A D—

OINK!

...A PIG.

GRNT! GRNT!

I SAID THE PIGS LOOKED TASTY AT THIS PART-TIME GIG, AND THEY GAVE ME ONE AS PAYMENT IN COMMODITIES.

CUUUTE!!
WHAT'S ITS NAME?
ISN'T IT A BERK-SHIRE?
NOT THE BREED NAME.
ITS NAME IS "FORMER PREZ"!
YOU DIDN'T EVEN THINK ABOUT IT!
I'M GONNA EAT IT ANYWAY. I DON'T NEED TO THINK UP A GOOD NAME!
WH...
YOU'RE GONNA EAT HIM?
YOU BET. BLACK PIGS ARE TASTY. LIKE KAGOSHIMA BLACK PORK. THAT'S FAMOUS, RIGHT?
TASTY!!
SUPER TASTY!!!!

I SEE...SO FORMER PREZ WILL BE TURNED INTO SAUSAGE EVENTUALLY.
NO, WE SHOULD TURN FORMER PREZ INTO BACON.
BLACK PORK? THEN FORMER PREZ WOULD MAKE GOOD DEEP-FRIED PORK CUTLETS.
PORK BOWLS ...
LET'S TURN FORMER PREZ INTO MINCEMEAT.
NONE FOR YOU, YODA.
ANYWAY, KEEPING THE PIG WAS FINE AND DANDY AT FIRST, BUT I DON'T REALLY HAVE SPACE.
AND SINCE I UP AND GRADUATED, IT'S NOT LIKE I CAN KEEP A PIG AT EZO AG EITHER.
HMM... SO YOU NEED LAND...?
driver's license
still can't find a buyer for our land cuz it's so rough and by the mountains
I KNOW SOMEONE WITH LAND...
NICE!! HOOK ME UP!!
BUT IT'S PRETTY FAR AWAY, AND IT'S IN THE MOUNTAINS, AND IT'S NOT MAINTAINED, AND SINCE IT'S FARMLAND, THE LEGAL ASPECT WITH SUCCESSION AND STUFF MIGHT BE A HASSLE.

A HASSLE!?
I WANT TO EAT SOME GOOD PORK THE EASY WAY!!
IF YOU WANT TO EAT GOOD FOOD, YOU CAN'T SKIMP ON TIME AND EFFORT!!
HOW ABOUT IF I JUST PUT THE PIG OUT TO PASTURE!?
OOH!
PASTURE-RAISED PORK!! THAT SOUNDS GOOD!!

CAN WE LAUNCH A BUSINESS WITH THIS PIG AS THE STARTING POINT!?
IF YOU PASTURE PIGS IN THE WILD, THEY'RE MORE LIKELY TO GET PARASITES!!
WOULD IT BE PROFIT-ABLE!?
NO, COME ON, THEY'D GET EATEN BY BEARS!
WACHA WACHA WACHA (CLAMOR) WACHA WACHA WACHA
YOU OVER THERE!! PAY ATTENTION TO MY HEROIC EXPLOITS!!
BUWAWA (BWOOSH)
BUBUUU (B-BZZZZ)
Minami-kujou-san is out of time.

The Tale of Keiji Tokiwa, Shinnosuke Aikawa, and Tamako Inada

YOU WANT TO TEAM UP WITH OOKAWA-SENPAI!? DON'T!!

THAT GUY IS CLEARLY A NEGATIVE! HE BLEW UP YOUR ROOM!
NOTHIN' GOOD'LL COME OF IT.
OOKAWA-SAN LOOKS LIKE A POSITIVE ASSET AT FIRST GLANCE SINCE HE'S GOOD AT BUILDING ALL SORTS OF THINGS... YOU'D NEVER SUSPECT IT...
YOU HAVE ZERO CAPITAL NOW, RIGHT?
A ZERO MULTIPLIED BY ANYTHING IS STILL A ZERO.
MMMRNGH... GETTING INTO THE PIG BUSINESS CALLS TO ME, THOUGH...
WUT, WUT, WUUUT!? YOU'RE GONNA START A BUSINESS WITH PIGS!? SOUNDS FUN!!
AH, IT'S MINUS MAN.
MULTIPLYING A NEGATIVE AND A NEGATIVE RESULTS IN A POSITIVE!?
AH!
THAT ONLY WORKS IN THE WORLD OF MATH!
CALM. DOWN.
USING ABANDONED FARMLAND IS A PRETTY GOOD IDEA, THOUGH.
WON'T PREPARING THE LAND BE A HASSLE?
THERE'S THIS METHOD CALLED "HOOF CULTIVATION."
YOU HAVE CATTLE SMOOTH OUT UNEVEN, OVERGROWN LAND.

YOU RELEASE THE COWS OUT INTO MOUNTAIN LAND OR ABANDONED LAND—PLACES FARM EQUIPMENT CAN'T ACCESS.
COWS WILL EAT BAMBOO GRASS AND EVEN TWIGS AND SO ON WHEN THEY'RE HUNGRY, AND SINCE THEY WEIGH SO MUCH, THEY'LL TRAMPLE THE UNEVEN LAND FLAT.
THE ABANDONED LAND GETS CLEARED, AND THE COWS' LEG MUSCLES GET A WORKOUT, MAKING THEM HEALTHIER.
THEN ONCE THE LAND IS LEVEL, YOU SOW SEEDS FOR PASTURE GRASS.
AIKAWA, WHAT'S YOUR PROJECT AGAIN? ANIMAL WELFARE?
RIGHT.
RESEARCHING METHODS THAT RELIEVE THE STRESS ON BOTH FARM OPERATORS AND THEIR LIVESTOCK, IN A NICE BALANCE.
THIS HOOF CULTIVATION METHOD...COULD YOU USE DAIRY COWS WHOSE MILK YIELD HAS DECREASED? ONES THAT ARE ABOUT TO GET SOLD FOR SLAUGHTER?
CULLED COWS?
I WONDER...

I'D REALLY LIKE TO GIVE SOME VALUE TO THE REJECTED ANIMALS TOO...
...YEAH. THAT'S A NICE IDEA.
INADA-SAN, AFTER HOW MANY DELIVERIES DOES YOUR FARM CULL COWS ON AVERAGE?
AFTER THREE OR FOUR CALVING AND LACTATION CYCLES, WE SELL THEM OFF FOR SLAUGHTER.
SOME FARMS PASTURE THEIR RETIRED WAGYU COWS IN THE MOUNTAINS AND FORESTS TO IMPROVE THEIR TASTE BEFORE SHIPPING THEM OUT FOR MEAT.
IF CULLED HOLSTEINS COULD PRODUCE A TASTE ON PAR WITH WAGYU BEEF, I THINK THAT WOULD ADD VALUE TO THEM.
W
H
SOME PEOPLE SAY COWS THAT HAVE CALVED HAVE A STRONGER TASTE.
PEOPLE GENERALLY ASSOCIATE RETIRED DAIRY COW BEEF WITH INFERIOR TASTE. IF YOU WERE TO MAKE A BUSINESS OF IT, YOU'D HAVE AN OPENING THERE.
NOT MANY OTHERS ARE DOING IT, SEE.
THAT IS AN OPPORTUNITY...

WE HAVE TO SELL OUR CULLED COWS AT AN UNREASONABLY LOW PRICE. IF WE CAN ADD VALUE TO THEM, IT WOULD BE A HUGE FINANCIAL GAIN!!
BUT WOULD IT WORK?
CAN IT ADD ENOUGH VALUE TO BE WORTH THE EXTRA COSTS?
DOES EXERCISING COWS MAKE THE BEEF TASTIER?
THEY END UP WITH LESS EXCESS FAT.
COULD GO OVER WELL WITH PEOPLE WHO PREFER LEAN BEEF?
BEEF!
THEY'RE TALKIN' ABOUT BEEF!
COULD YOU SELL IT AS A HEALTH-CONSCIOUS PRODUCT?
HMMM...
THE INSTANT YOU TALK ABOUT EATING BEEF, CAN IT EVEN COUNT AS "HEALTHY"?
COULD IT BEAT CHEAP IMPORTED LEAN BEEF?
HMMM...
HMMM...
GUIDANCE COUNSELOR
A SHORT-TERM STUDY ABROAD!?
THAT'S RIGHT. WE HAVE AN ARRANGEMENT WHERE WE SEND ONE STUDENT WITH OUTSTANDING GRADES FROM EACH PROGRAM TO A HIGH SCHOOL ABROAD FOR A ONE-TO TWO-WEEK TRIAL EXPERIENCE.
YOUR GRADES ARE BEST IN YOUR PROGRAM BY A LONG SHOT. I WANTED TO SEE HOW YOU'D FEEL ABOUT IT.

ABROAD...
A HIGH SCHOOL ABROAD...?
THAT'S SCARY, BUT...IT MIGHT BE PRETTY COOL.
OH, SO YOU'RE INTERESTED?
WANT TO GO?
IT'S A FARM SCHOOL IN FRANCE...
FRANCE!?
THAT'S RIGHT, THE AGRICULTURAL POWERHOUSE.
YOU MIGHT GAIN SOME GOOD INSIGHTS FOR STARTING YOUR BUSINESS.
FRANCE...
I...I WOULD LIKE TO GO, BUT CAN I PASS THIS OPPORTUNITY TO ANOTHER PERSON, SIR?
WHY? THIS EXPERIENCE WOULD BE GOOD FOR YOUR FUTURE.

THERE'S SOMEONE WHOSE FUTURE COULD BENEFIT EVEN MORE FROM THE EXPERIENCE THAN MINE.

The Tale of Mayumi Yoshino

FRANCE!!
THE HOME OF CHEESE!!
YES!! I'LL ABSOLUTELY GO!!

IT'S SETTLED, THEN.
DO YOU KNOW ENOUGH ENGLISH OR FRENCH FOR SIMPLE CONVERSATIONS?
NO PROBLEM!!!

BOOK: THE ROSE OF VERSAILLES: THE TALE OF FORBIDDEN LOVE *BY RIYOKO IKEDA*

GOOOO (ROAR)
WOW. YOSHINO'S MADE OF STRONG STUFF, DOING SOMETHING LIKE THIS.
YOSHINO OFF IN FRANCE!!
WELL, SHE'LL PROBABLY BE ABLE TO COMMUNICATE, EVEN IF IT'S IN BROKEN ENGLISH...
OH MY GOSH! THIS IS SUPER GOOD!!
AND IT TEACHES YOU HISTORY!!
IT SPREAD POSITIVELY TO MIKAGE TOO. I'M GLAD.
A FISH OUT OF WATER CHUCKED INTO A TOTALLY NEW WORLD—DÉJÀ VU, RIGHT?
WA HA HA HA!
TAKES ME BACK TO MYSELF A YEAR AGO!
GOOD LUCK, YOSHINO...
SET FORTH TO BECOME A CHEESE-MAKER ...!!
AIR FRANCE

<Welcome to Normandy Agricultural High School, Mayumi!>
THANK YOU FOR HOSTING ME!
<Let's get straight to the good stuff. This is our school's pride and joy!>
AWE-SOME! A CHEESE PLANT!?

<At our school, we keep and sell all kinds of aquarium fish.>
BITAN (SMACK)
びたん
<Many of our alumni work in pet shops.>
<We do practical hands-on lessons so they'll be able to work in the field immediately after graduation.>
<Oh, we even have Japanese koi in that tank over there!>
CHARARAN (JINGLE) CHARARAN
ちゃらん ちゃらん
AH! IT'S A MESSAGE FROM YOSHINO!
Help.
Yoshino
!!?

Silver Spoon

YUUSHI MIKAGE

AKI MIKAGE'S UNCLE

Chapter 99
Tale of Four Seasons②

SFX: WAI (CLAMOR) WAI
HEY, YOSHINO! YOU'RE BACK!
YOUR JOINTS ARE LOOKING WEIRD, YOSHINO!!
HOW WAS FRANCE?
WERE THERE HOT GUYS?
GIVE ME A SOU-VENIR!
...I DID NOTHING BUT TAKE CARE OF FISH THE WHOLE TIME.
FISH?
NOT COWS?

WHAT DID YOU EVEN GO TO A FRENCH FARM SCHOOL FOR?
SO YOU DIDN'T GET TO STUDY CHEESE?
I-I-I-I-I PUSHED YOU TO GO TO FRANCE WITH GOOD INTENTIONS, I SWEAR. WAS IT ACTUALLY, LIKE, THE LAST THING YOU NEEDED!!?
DOO (SHUDDER)
SORRY, YOSHINO... I SCREWED UP...
NO.
WHILE I WAS IN FRANCE, I ATE CHEESE FOR THREE MEALS A DAY PLUS SNACKS. I GOT TONS OF FLAVOR INPUT.
UH...
EVERY MEAL AND SNACKS?
URP...
THANKS TO THAT, I HAVE A DEFINITE SENSE OF THE FLAVOR I SHOULD SHOOT FOR NOW!

KOFUKU
PATRIOTISM
HAPPINESS
Chapter 99:
Tale of Four Seasons ②
KOFUKU STATION

The Tale of Aki Mikage

HEY.
HEYA.
MRR HRR HRN!
OH? DOING COMPOSITION TODAY?
SHORT ESSAYS.
IT'S PRACTICE FOR THE RECOMMENDATION EXAM.
MODERN JAPANE
WE'LL BE GIVEN THE TOPIC ON EXAMINATION DAY, AND WE'LL HAVE NINETY MINUTES TO WRITE AN ESSAY ABOUT ONE THOUSAND CHARACTERS LONG.
SAKURAGI-SENSEI TOLD ME TO PRACTICE AND GAVE ME SOME TOPICS.
I THINK I'LL END UP WRITING A FEW EVERY MONTH...
OH, SO YOU CAN COPE NO MATTER WHAT TOPIC YOU GET?
GETTING IN ON RECOMMENDATION SOUNDS SURPRISINGLY TOUGH.
OUR STRATEGY IS TO INCORPORATE MY INTERESTS, SO AS LONG AS I CAN LINK IT BACK TO HORSES, I CAN MANAGE.
...THERE! ALL DONE COPYING DOWN MY FINAL DRAFT!!

I HOPE NOTHING'S WRONG WITH IT...
CAN I SEE?
......
YOU'RE SPELLING OUT TOO MANY WORDS WHERE YOU SHOULD BE USING KANJI.
......I THOUGHT I COULD PAD OUT THE CHARACTER COUNT...
...EH HEH...
WHAT'LL HAPPEN IF YOU WATER DOWN MILK SHIPMENTS?
I'LL BE KILLED. GOT IT.
I'LL REDO IT.
OKAY, TIME TO START CLUB!
DO YOUR WARM-UPS!
ALL RIGHT.
'KAY.

READ THE NEWS-PAPER EVERY DAY.
THEY REGULARLY COVER ISSUES THAT COULD BE ESSAY TOPICS.
I SEE!
THEY'RE AS CLOSE AS THAT, AND THEY AREN'T GOING OUT, YOU KNOW.
NYU (SWOOP)
DWUH!? TH...THEY AREN'T!? I JUST ASSUMED ...!!
PSST! PSST! PSST! PSST! PSST!
I KNOW, RIGHT? IT'S SO WEIRD, RIGHT?
PSST! PSST! PSST! PSST! PSST!
SO ON THAT SUBJECT...
MRMR... MRMR... MRMR... MRMR... MRMR...
M-ME!? BUT I CAN'T ...
YES, YOU CAN! GO!! SENPAI'S ORDERS!!
EXCUSE ME... ERM...
HACHIKEN-SENPAI, MIKAGE-SENPAI...
?

"IT'S OBVIOUS TO EVERYONE THAT YOU BOTH LIKE EACH OTHER, SO HOW COME YOU AREN'T GOING OUT? WHAT'S THE DEAL WITH THAT?"
馬術
LOOK, I PROMISED MIKAGE'S DAD I'D TUTOR HER UNTIL SHE GETS INTO COLLEGE!!
HE SAYS HE'LL MURDER ME IF I USE IT AS A PRETEXT TO MAKE A MOVE ON HER!!
DATING HER IS A HUGE NO-NO!!
MRMR...
MRMR...
MRMR...
MRMR...
MRMR...
MM-HMM.
MM-HMM.
MM-HMM.
MM-HMM.
AHEM...
ERM...

"HE ONLY SAID *YOU* CAN'T MAKE A MOVE ON *HER*, HACHIKEN-SENPAI.
"COULDN'T MIKAGE-SENPAI BE THE ONE TO MAKE THE FIRST MOVE!?"
...IS WHAT SAKAE-SENPAI SAID TO ASK...
FORGET IT...
I BET YOU THINK I'M A HUGE WIMP TOO...
WHA!?
N-N-N-NO...
HOLDING IN YOUR FEELINGS WHILE YOU TUTOR HER SO YOU WON'T INTERFERE WITH MIKAGE-SAN'S COLLEGE ENTRANCE EXAM PREP...
IT'S LIKE, WOW, YOU MUST REALLY CARE ABOUT HER A WHOLE LOT!!
I...I-I-I THINK THAT'S REALLY COOL!!

SHE JUST INCREASED HACHIKEN'S MARKET VALUE WHILE AT THE SAME TIME TYING HIM DOWN TIGHT!
SINCE HACHIKEN IS SUCH A RESPONSIBLE GOODY TWO-SHOES, THIS MAKES IT EVEN HARDER FOR HIM TO MAKE A MOVE...
MY HEART GOES OUT TO THE GUY...
MIKAGE-SAAAN.
YES!?
ABOUT THE HOOF CULTIVATION EXPERIMENT FOR OUR ANIMAL WELFARE PROJECT...
...COME TALK TO MINAMI-SENSEI WITH ME LATER.
OKAY. SURE THING!
OH! YOU'RE DOING THAT SO SOON?
REMEMBER THE COW YOU HELPED DELIVER LAST YEAR?
OH, THAT CALF?
BLURGH...
WE WANT TO PASTURE YOUNGER COWS WITH THE CULLED COWS TOO TO COMPARE DATA.
DO YOU MIND IF WE USE YOUR COW?
MY COW COULD BE USEFUL!?
YEAH. MINAMI-SENSEI ALREADY GAVE US THE OKAY...
SURE!!
PLEASE USE MY COW!!

GIT!!
PESHI (SMACK)
ぺしっ
MOO!

Animal Welfare Team
Farming Bonds Business Team
Joint Experiment Site
1129 Ezo Ag Howcan Thatbe
1305 Ezo Ag Goget Them
0081 Ezo Ag Yuugo Eight
WE'RE ALL SET!
I HOPE IT GOES WELL.
YEAH.
PUT YOUR BEST HOOF FORWARD...
MY COW...!
2D
八軒
0081
SUN (SNIFF)
SUN すんすん

UH-OH!!
THAT'S NOT GOOD.
WHAT IS IT?
ACONITE.
ズボ
ZUBO (RIP)
IT'S POI-SON-OUS.
IT GROWS PRETTY COMMONLY IN THE WILD AROUND HERE. IF YOU SEE ANY, GET RID OF IT.
UHHH, HOW BAD IS IT IF A COW EATS THAT...?
THEIR EYES'LL GO VACANT.
OR THEY'LL FOAM FROM THE MOUTH.
OR THEY'LL DIE.
MY COWWW!!!

Komaba Ranch
HEYA, ICHIROU. YOU GETTIN' ALONG OKAY?
YES, SIR.
Mikage Ranch 御影牧場
Y'ALL FOUND A BUYER FOR YOUR PASTURE LAND YET?
NOT YET, SIR.
LAND THIS DEEP IN THE MOUNTAINS AIN'T EASY TO USE, AND SINCE NOBODY'LL BUY IT, IT'S ALL OVERGROWN.
THEY'LL BEAT THE PRICE EVEN LOWER ON US.
I SEE...

'BOUT YOUR LAND...
YES?
THE OVER-GROWN PASTURE LAND Y'ALL AIN'T USIN'.
I'M THINKIN' OF RENTIN' IT FROM YA.
I WANNA MILK OUR COWS MORE TIMES PER DAY TO PAY OFF DEBT.
BUT THAT'LL MEAN FEEDIN' 'EM MORE.
SO I FIGURE WE OUGHTA RENT YOUR LAND AND HAVE THE COWS GRAZE THERE.
IF YOU'LL BE MOWING IT FROM TIME TO TIME, THE LAND'LL STAY NEAT TOO. IT'S MORE THAN WE COULD EVER ASK FOR!
THEN I'LL COME BY LATER TO TALK TO YOUR MA.
HERE I'VE GOT YOU STANDING AROUND... PLEASE, COME IN!
YEP.

HELLO, UNCLE MIKAGE!
HEY, NINO, MISORA. Y'ALL STUDYING?
GOOD GIRLS!
COME TA THINK OF IT, YOU GUYS'VE BEEN STUDYIN' A LOT THESE DAYS.
SINCE WE DON'T HAVE FARM WORK NOW, WE'VE GOT LOTS OF TIME!
R... RIGHT...
BUT THAT'S ONLY ONE REASON.
WE BOTH WANT TO GO TO COLLEGE.
YUP. I'LL SEND YA THERE.
I'LL WORK HARD AND SAVE UP YOUR TUITIONS—
NO, THANKS.

WE'LL GO ON SCHOLARSHIPS.
IF WE GET GOOD GRADES, WE CAN GET SCHOLARSHIPS WE WON'T HAFTA PAY BACK, RIGHT?
WE'LL GO TO A GOOD COLLEGE AND GET GOOD JOBS.
WE'LL TAKE CARE OF YOU AND MOM!
WA-HA-HA-HA!! YOU'VE GOT YOURSELF SOME DEPENDABLE KID SISTERS!!
NINO, MISORA, I BROUGHT YA MILK AND VEGGIES FROM OUR FARM.
DRINK UP, EAT UP, AND STUDY UP!
YAAAY!!
MILK!
MILK!

YOUR WILD LAND...
AKI SENT THIS OVER.
SAYS IT'S A PROJECT SHE'S DOIN' WITH HACHIKEN AN' THEIR FRIENDS AT SCHOOL.
THEY'VE ONLY JUST STARTED, SO IT AIN'T COMPLETE YET. IT'S INTRIGUING STUFF, THOUGH.
Restoring Wildland & Adding Value to Culled Cows Via Hoof Cultivation
IS IT JUST ME, OR IS AKI GIVIN' MORE SERIOUS THOUGHT TO FARMING SINCE SHE DECIDED NOT TO TAKE OVER THE FARM?
THAT'S THE IRONY OF IT.

workbook
workbook
THANK YOU.
YEP.
PWAAH!
MIKAGE RANCH MILK IS SO GOOD!!
AIN'T IT?
BUT OUR MILK IS EVEN BETTER!
WHAT!?
IT'S TRUE. OURS IS TASTIER.
NOT YOU TOO, ICHI-ROU!?
THE FAT'S A LITTLE HEAVY.
WHY, YOU!! YOU'RE ON!!
PAY OFF THAT DEBT FAST AND KEEP COWS AGAIN, YOU SON OF A GUN!!!

Silver Spoon

Chapter 100:

Tale of Four Seasons ③

... YOU'RE BOTH MAKING SCARY FACES...
OUR PROPOSAL STILL CAN'T GET THE OKAY.
I KNEW GETTING CAPITAL FOR A BUSINESS WITH NO RECORD, NO BRAND, NO NOTHING WOULD BE AN UPHILL BATTLE, BUT REALITY IS EVEN HARSHER...
LET ME SEE.
GNNNN...!!
YOU'RE ASKING YOUR DAD FOR AN INVEST-MENT, RIGHT?
NOT FOR A LOAN?
RIGHT.
WITH LENDING, ONCE YOU FINISH PAYING OFF THE LOAN, YOUR RELATIONSHIP WITH THAT PERSON IS JUST OVER.
BUT IF THEY'RE INVESTING, WHEN YOU MAKE A PROFIT, YOU CAN PAY DIVIDENDS TO THE PERSON WHO INVESTED MONEY IN YOU, RIGHT?

PERSONALLY, I THINK IT'S MORE MOTIVATING THAT WAY.
THOUGH THEY CAN MEDDLE IN YOUR MANAGEMENT THEN.
IF YOU HAVE ANY THOUGHTS ABOUT OUR PROPOSAL, COULD YOU TELL US? ANYTHING AT ALL.
HMMM...I WOULDN'T UNDERSTAND THE COMPLICATED PARTS.
AN AGRICULTURAL BUSINESS WHERE EVERYONE WORKS TOGETHER TO MAKE UP FOR THE AREAS WHERE THEY FALL SHORT AS INDIVIDUALS...
MM-HMM, HELPING ONE ANOTHER IS IMPORTANT. BUT THAT SAID...
...DON'T RUSH INTO CO-SIGNING ANY LOANS.
KOKU (NOD)
KOKU
KOKU
KOKU
KOKU

I HEARD ALL ABOUT IT, AKI MIKAGE!!!
AYAME-CHAN! WHAT'S UP?
YOU HOPE TO ATTEND OOEZO UNIVERSITY OF ANIMAL HUSBANDRY, I HEAR?
WHERE DID YOU HEAR THAT?
MY GRANDPAPA IS THE FARMING CO-OP'S UNION PRESIDENT! NATURALLY, WHEN IT COMES TO INFO ON THE MEMBERS, I'M PRIVY TO ALL KINDS OF... (ETC.)
I'LL GET TO THE POINT! THE GAME IS ON, AKI MIKAGE!!

FIRST, WE'LL VIE FOR SUPREMACY ON THE CENTER TEST!!
ZUBA (BLUNT)
ZUBAN
OH, I'M HOPING FOR A RECOMMENDATION.
...WHAT DO YOU MEAN? YOU DON'T HAVE TO TAKE THE CENTER TEST?
THAT'S SO LUCKY... MAYBE I SHOULD TRY FOR A RECOMMENDATION TOO...
IF SHE GOT A RECOMMENDATION, WOULD THAT MEAN SHE'D BE COMPETING WITH YOU?
SINCE I GO TO A FARM SCHOOL, I'M IN RECOMMENDATION CATEGORY "A."
AYAME-CHAN GOES TO A GENERAL HIGH SCHOOL, SO SHE'D BE IN CATEGORY "B."
I'LL JUST GET DOWN...
CATEGORY "A" HAS TWENTY SLOTS, AND CATEGORY "B" HAS FORTY SLOTS.
OH! IF THERE ARE TWICE AS MANY SPACES AVAILABLE TO ME, THAT'S A CAKEWALK!!
THE REQUIRED GPA FOR CATEGORY "B" IS AT LEAST 4.0, I THINK?
IS YOUR GPA HIGH ENOUGH?
HO-HO-HO-HO-HO! A FOOLISH QUESTION!!

MY REPORT CARDS ARE GRACED ONLY BY BEAUTIFUL NUMBERS !!
NAMELY, THE #1 NUMBER! "ONE" !!!
A GRAND DECLARATION THAT SHE GETS ALL ONES!!!
MY PHYS ED GRADE IS A FIVE!!
URK!! I LOST!!
IF YOU APPLY BY RECOMMENDATION, YOU HAVE TO WRITE A PERSONAL STATEMENT.
WRITING SOMETHING TO SELL YOURSELF, YES?
EASY AS PIE!
SARA さら SARA さら SARA (SWISH) さら
VOILA!
Admitting me, a student with a promising future, is for the good of your school.
YUP! YOU'D FLUNK!

THERE'S ALSO AN ESSAY.
THEY GIVE YOU THE TOPIC THE DAY OF THE TEST, AND YOU WRITE A THOUSAND-CHARACTER ESSAY ON IT.
BY THE WAY, THE TOPICS OVER THE LAST FEW YEARS WERE...
WRITE ABOUT ONGOIN EFFORTS TO REDUCE GREENHOUS S EMISSIONS IN JAPAN'S AGRICULTUR AND LIVESTOCK INDUSTRIES, CHOOSING ROM THE FOLLOWING KEYWORDS: ETHANO BIODIESEL, FOOD WASTE, LIVESTOCK WASTE, METHANE." "THE EFFECTS OF TRAD BERALIZATION SUCH AS THE TPP ON JAPA AGRICULTURE INDUSTRY. KEYWORDS: FOO SELF-SUFFICIENCY RATE, REGIONAL ECONO AGRICULTURAL PROTECTIONISM, FOOD SAFE LARGE-SCALE FARMING, SPECIAL INTEREST "SUPPOSE YOU ARE JAPAN'S MINISTER O AGRICULTURE, FORESTRY, AND FISHERIE APART FROM OF TRADE POLICIES, WHAT SOLUTIONS WOULD YOU PUT IN PLAC TO ADDRESS CURRENT CHALLENGES FACING THE AGRICULTURAL INDUST
YOU CAN'T RUN AWAY.
YOU'VE GOTTEN STRONGER, AKI MIKAGE...
I HAVE NOTHING LEFT TO TEACH YOU...
WHO DO YOU THINK YOU ARE?
TO GO TO OOEZO U, YOU'D HAVE TO WORK LIKE YOUR LIFE DEPENDS ON IT, STARTING NOW...
YOU SHOULD START CRAM SCHOOL OR GET A HOME TUTOR AND REALLY HIT THE BOOKS.
CRAM SCHOOL!? WE LIVE IN THE MOUNTAINS! WE DON'T HAVE ANYTHING LIKE THAT!!

OH!
AN ONLINE TUTOR!
OH YEAH! I DO KNOW AN ONLINE TUTOR!
WHAT!? INTRODUCE ME!
HELLO, BRO?
I WANT TO INTRODUCE A POTENTIAL CLIENT TO YOU.
Nice! I'd love to have 'em! Thanks much!
DO YOU REMEMBER THE FLASHY GIRL FROM THE HORSE-RIDING MEET?
WITH THE RINGLETS. AYAME MINAMI-KUJOU.
A HIGH SCHOOL SECOND-YEAR.
YEAH.
OOEZO UNIVERSITY OF ANIMAL HUS-BANDRY.
SAYS SHE WANTS TO TAKE THEIR EXAM TO COMPETE WITH MIKAGE.

Hey, as long as she wants to study, the reason doesn't matter!
WA HA HA HA!
BY THE WAY, HER GRADES ARE A CLEAN SWEEP OF ONES ACROSS THE BOARD.
...Uh?
GOOD LUCK.
Wait... but it's the summer of her second y—
WORK LIKE YOUR LIFE DE-PENDS ON IT.
DIFFERENT RECOMMENDATION CATEGORIES OR NOT, IF YOU FLUNK THAT APPLICATION, YOU'RE SWITCHING TO GENERAL ADMISSIONS, RIGHT?
HO-HO-HO-HO-HO!
MY THANKS!
IT'S LIKE YOU'RE GIVING YOUR COMPETITION A LEG UP. IS THAT SUCH A GOOD IDEA?
DO YOU THINK SO?
AYAME-CHAN JUST HAS THIS BOTTOMLESS POSITIVITY, RIGHT?
...
I GET SO MUCH ENERGY FROM HER.

I HOPE WE BOTH GET IN!
H... HEY, SO...
WHEN YOU GET INTO COLLEGE... Y'KNOW...
ERM ...
I'LL ASK YOU OFFICIALLY, SO...!
WILL YOU...!
G...
G-G-G-G-G- GO OU—

GO UP!
GON (BONK)
I DROP BY DURING OUR WALK, AND THIS IS WHAT YOU'RE UP TO? YOU ANIMAL!
I'M SORRY. I'M SORRY. I'M SORRY. I'M SORRY FOR GETTING CARRIED AWAY.
HI, OOKAWA-SENPAI.
GUI GUI GUI (SHOVE)
GOSH, FORMER PREZ HAS GOTTEN BIG.
SNRT! GRNT!
'COS I KNOW HOW TO RAISE 'EM.
DO YOU WALK FORMER PREZ EVERY DAY?
YOU BET.
HOW IS IT A GUY THIS METHODICAL CAN'T GET HIRED?
I SEE... SO FORMER PREZ WILL BE TURNED INTO MEAT SOON...
GRNT!
YEAH, ABOUT THAT...

AS WE'VE BEEN GOING ON WALKS LIKE THIS, I'VE COME TO REALIZE I'D REALLY RATHER NOT EAT THIS PIG...
RH!
GRNT!
AHH, SO YOU GOT ATTACHED?
I TOTALLY GET IT. PIGS ARE SO SMART AND CUTE.
NO, FORMER PREZ REMINDED ME OF SOMETHING—PIGS ARE OMNIVORES.
I'VE SEEN THIS PIG EATING DISGUSTING THINGS OFF THE GROUND. I CAN'T UNSEE IT.
WHEN I THINK OF PIGS' MEAT BEING MADE OF [redacted] AND [redacted], I LOSE MY APPETITE.
MWA.
IF PIGS GET TOO BIG, THE FLAVOR OF THE MEAT DECREASES, YOU KNOW. IT'D BE A LOT OF WORK TO TAKE CARE OF A FULL-GROWN PIG TOO.
HRRM...I DO WANT TO EAT PIGS. I JUST DON'T WANT TO EAT THIS ONE...

...I SEE THIS ONE'S FEMALE...
かり かり KARI KARI (SCRTCH)
COULD SHE BE A BROOD SOW?
GRNT!
MIKAGE, DO YOU KNOW ANY LAND WHERE I COULD KEEP A FAMILY OF PIGS!?
WE STOPPED KEEPING HORSES, SO THE LAND WE USED FOR THEIR PASTURE IS FREE...
MUL-TIPLY AND EAT THEM!?
ZUKYUUN (BAZING)
BUT IT DOES GET BEARS A LOT.
BEWARE OF BEARS
WHY SHOULD MY DREAMS HAVE TO BE DASHED BY SOME STUPID BEARS!?

I WANT TO MAKE THIS PIG THE "EVE" OF PIG EDEN!
HOW WILL YOU HANDLE THE MATING?
WILL YOU KEEP A MALE PIG TOO?
THERE SHOULD BE SUPPLIERS WHO SELL PIG SPERM.
I THINK THEY EVEN SEND IT TO YOU VIA DELIVERY SERVICE...
HUH!? MAIL-ORDER ADAM!?
THAT REMINDS ME. IN THE PAST, FARM FAMILIES WOULD KEEP PIGS JUST FOR THE FAMILY TO EAT...
WHEN THEY WANTED TO BREED THEM, THEY'D HAVE A BREEDING BOAR BROUGHT IN AND MATE WITH THEIR SOWS.
LIVESTOCK MANAGEMENT WING
THE ESTRUS CYCLE OF ADULT FEMALE PIGS IS TWENTY-ONE DAYS, AND THEIR GESTATION PERIOD IS 114 DAYS.
INCLUDING THE NURSING PERIOD, THEY CAN HAVE A LITTER TWICE A YEAR.
BERK-SHIRES HAVE LITTERS OF SEVEN TO EIGHT PIGLETS, SO...
...YOU COULD EAT FIFTEEN PIGS A YEAR!!

...COULD A BUSINESS BE BUILT OFF OF THIS?
PASTURE-RAISED PORK?
RAISING PIGS IN AND OF ITSELF IS EASY.
LEAVE THEM ALONE IN NATURE, AND THEY'LL THRIVE ON THEIR OWN.
ONLY, IF YOU WANT TO SELL THEM, YOU'LL HAVE TO CONSIDER DISEASE CONTROL, FEED, SLAUGHTER-HOUSES, AND SO ON AND SO FORTH.
TO MAKE THEM A PRODUCT, YOU'D HAVE TO MAINTAIN A REGULAR STANDARD OF QUALITY.
THE FEED GIVEN TO BREEDING PIGS AND PORK PIGS IS DIFFERENT.
COULD YOU USE THE ACORNS THAT WE GET AROUND HERE?
LIKE WHAT THEY FEED IBERIAN PIGS?
FIRST SHE HELPED WITH THE FUND, NOW THIS— YOU CAN ALWAYS COUNT ON FUJI-SENSEI.
YEAH.
THANKS FOR ALWAYS GOING ALONG WITH MY HAREBRAINED IDEAS.
NO BOTHER AT ALL.
I DO IT BECAUSE I ENJOY IT TOO.
BESIDES...
...I'LL ONLY GET TO TEACH YOU KIDS FOR A LITTLE LONGER NOW...

I'LL BE...
...SAYING GOOD-BYE TO THIS SCHOOL AFTER THIS YEAR.
FUJI-SENSEI, YOU'RE LEAVING EZO AG!?
MM.
WHY? ARE YOU TRANSFERRING TO ANOTHER SCHOOL?
HEH...
AT MY AGE... WELL...
HUH ...?
OH!!
SHE'S GETTING MARRIED!?

CON-GRAT-ULA...
I'M GOING TO BECOME A HUNTER.
IN RECENT YEARS, THE HOKKAIDO DEER POPULATION HAS EXPLODED. THE FINANCIAL LOSSES FROM THE CROP DAMAGE ARE NO LAUGHING MATTER.
IT SEEMS THERE ARE TOO FEW YOUNG HUNTERS, SO I'VE DECIDED TO DIVE INTO A CAREER CHANGE!
WE SEE
BETTER TO DO IT WHILE I'M STILL YOUNG!
I SEE... I'LL MISS FUJI-SENSEI...
SHE'S TAUGHT ME A LOT...

OH! SENSEI! WE GET BEARS IN OUR FIELDS A LOT. IT'S A REAL PROBLEM!
YOU KNOW WHO TO CALL!
OMIGOSH! FUJI-SENSEI, SO MANLY!!
YOU CAN REALLY COUNT ON HER!!
SO YOU'RE LEAVING...
WE'LL CERTAINLY MISS YOU AROUND HERE...
LIVESTOCK MANAGEMENT WING
I WON'T BE A SALARIED EMPLOYEE, SO MY INCOME WON'T BE STABLE. BUT LIVING THE LIFE OF A HUNTER HAS BEEN MY DREAM FOR A WHILE NOW.
IF YOU BAG ANY DEER, GIVE US SOME MEAT!
THAT'S A DARING MOVE!
I'M A BIT EMBARRASSED TO BE CHASING DREAMS AT MY AGE.

WATCHING THESE KIDS TRYING TO START STUDENT BUSINESSES OR BRING THEIR GRADES UP FROM THE BOTTOM TO SHOOT FOR A NATIONAL COLLEGE...
IT GOT ME THINKING I STILL HAVE MORE IN ME TOO.
IT SEEMS WE FACULTY STILL HAVE MUCH TO LEARN FROM OUR OWN STUDENTS!
HA-HA-HA. COULDN'T HAVE PUT IT BETTER MYSELF!

Silver Spoon

KENTA ISHIYAMA

SHIMUKAPPU VILLAGE
KAMITOMAMU MIDDLE SCHOOL
AGRICULTURAL ENGINEERING
PROGRAM FIRST-YEAR

IN THE SAME RIDING
CLUB AS AKI MIKAGE
(KUMAUSHI RIDING CLUB),
TWO YEARS YOUNGER
THAN HER

EQUESTRIAN CLUB

A BIG PLOT OF LAND FOR PASTURING PIGS?
Chapter 101
Tale of Four Seasons ④
SURE, WE AREN'T USING IT.
SINCE THE HORSES ARE GONE, WE HAVE A WHOLE LOT OF EMPTY PASTURE.
IT'S OVER-GROWN WITH LOTS OF WEEDS. IS THAT ALL RIGHT?
MM-HMM. MM-HMM.
OH, THAT'S A NICE IDEA. MAYBE WE'LL TAKE A PIG TOO.
WE USED TO KEEP PIGS IN THE OLD DAYS. WE'D SLAUGHTER AND BUTCHER THEM OURSELVES.
YOUR GRANDPA'S SEEMED BORED EVER SINCE WE SOLD OFF THE HORSES. WHY DON'T YOU LET HIM TAKE CARE OF IT?

The only concern would be the bears, I suppose.
WE SHOULD BUILD A PIGSTY THE PIGS COULD ESCAPE INTO REAL FAST, RIGHT?
THE PIG'S OWNER IS PRETTY HANDY. I THINK HE'D BUILD IT HIMSELF.
All right. Then you should use the scrap and logs and other material we've got lying around here.
OKAY!
PATAN (SNAP)
SHE SAID WE CAN LEND YOU THE LAND!
AWESOME!! THANKS, MIKAGE!!
WHAT DOES THAT LEAVE? BREEDING FEES AND VACCINATION FEES? WAS THE SLAUGHTER-HOUSE EXPENSIVE TOO?
GUESS I'LL PUT MY PART-TIME WAGES INTO IT.
WHAT ABOUT THE MONEY FOR FEED?
THERE'S SPECIFIC FEED THAT'S SUITED TO PORK PIGS, RIGHT?

SINCE THEY'LL BE FOR OUR PERSONAL EATING FIRST, LET'S JUST LEAVE THEM OUT IN MOTHER NATURE AND SEE HOW IT TASTES.
ALL NATURAL, HUH? I BET INADA-SENPAI WOULD SNAP UP THAT IDEA.
ONCE I HAVE A UNIFORM TASTE AND STABLE PRODUCTION, YOUR COMPANY'S GOTTA SELL MY PRODUCT ALL OVER!
OH MAAAN... I'LL KEEP AT IT AND CREATE MY COMPANY AS SOON AS I CAN...
OHH, A BERKSHIRE!
HOT DIGGITY DOG!
"BLACK PIGS" AS THEY CALL 'EM, IS IT?
THE FAMOUS KAGOSHIMA BLACK PIGS ARE BERKSHIRES.
IF YOU FEED THEM POTATOES, THAT SHOULD IMPROVE THE MEAT QUALITY.
I CAN HARDLY WAIT.
GRNT!
SNRT!

PIGS ...
BOSO (MUMBLE)
ぼそ
NOW THAT TAKES ME BACK ...
IN THE OLD DAYS, WE KEPT PIGS TOO...
THEY'D BE OUR SPECIAL NEW YEAR'S MEAL...
もご MOGO (MMBL)
もご MOGO
OHH, THE MEMORIES... OUR CUTE PIGGIES...
WE WOULD DRIVE 'EM INTO A NARROW PASSAGE AND SWING AXES DOWN ON THE TOPS OF THEIR HEAD TO KILL 'EM...
IF YOU BUNGLED THE BLOW, THEY'D SQUEAL AND FLAIL LIKE DEMONS, AND THERE'D BE NO CONTROLLING 'EM THEN...
IT'D BE A SEA OF BLOOD AS FAR AS YOU COULD SEE...
もご MOGO
もご MOGO
UWAAH...

Chapter 101: Tale of Four Seasons ④

HOLY COW! I CAN BORROW ALL OF THIS LAND!?
PIGS LIKE TO PLAY IN THE MUD, SO BETTER MAKE 'EM A MUD PIT.
THEY'LL NEED A PLACE TO DRINK AND A PIGSTY TOO.
IF I CAN GET SOME SCRAP, I CAN BUILD IT.
SURE THING. C'MON OVER HERE.
AH...
THE STABLE...
NOT A SINGLE ONE OF THE HORSES I TOOK CARE OF IS HERE NOW...

Y'ALL CAN HAVE THIS.
BREAK IT DOWN AN' USE IT HOWEVER YA NEED.
OH NO, WE COULDN'T DESTROY IT! THE STABLE'S IMPORTANT TO YOU, RIGHT!?
WE DON'T GOT HORSES ANY-MORE.
AIN'T NO POINT IN KEEPIN' IT.
WHA ...
UNUSED BUILD-INGS FALL APART IN NO TIME.
BETTER TO HAVE SOMEBODY USE IT BEFORE THAT HAPPENS.
I'M SURE SHE'LL BE THRILLED TO BE USED TO HELP SOME YOUNG'NS DREAMS COME TRUE TOO.

TAKE 'ER FOR ME.
ALL RIGHT, AKI?
ぴしゃっ
PISHA (SMACK)
PILLARS, BEAMS, WALLS—ANYTHING YOU CAN USE, YOU GO AHEAD AND USE IT.

MIKAGE!
YOU OKAY WITH ME USING THIS?
YES!
ONE! TWO!
BARI (RIP)
BARI
BARI

DO (RMBL)
DO
DO
DO
DO
VUIIIIII (VREEE)
BARI (RIP)
BARI
BARI
YOU MAKIN' AN EXERCISE PEN FOR PIGS?
YUP.
HUH? THE STABLE...
GRANDPA SAID TO USE IT TO BUILD A PIGSTY.

I SEE...
HE LOOKS HAPPY, DOESN'T HE?
......
DON'T Y'ALL GET HURT.
OKAY!

YOU TWO HAVE SCHOOL TOMORROW, RIGHT?
IT'S A DAY OFF FOR ME, SO I'LL COME BACK HERE AND WORK ON IT TOMORROW TOO.
AH, OKAY.
BOTTLES: PASTURE TEA, 100% PEACH JUICE
THEN YOU OUGHTA STAY THE NIGHT.
IT'D BE A HASSLE TO GO BACK HOME EVERY TIME, RIGHT?
YOU DON'T MIND?
THE MIKAGES' HOME COOKING IS GREAT. YOU'LL OVEREAT. HECK, THEY'LL FORCE-FEED IT TO YOU.
NO JOKE?
I WANT TO BE PART OF THE MIKAGE FAMILY!
EH!? IS OOKAWA-KUN FROM AN ORDINARY FAMILY!?
GIRA (GLINT)
DO YOU THINK HE'D COME BE OUR SON-IN-LAW!?
NO WAY.
ALL RIGHT. LET'S GIVE IT ONE MORE PUSH!
OOF...

A FINE, HARD-WORKING YOUNG MAN LIKE THAT CAN'T GET A PERMANENT FULL-TIME JOB?
......
...I FIGURED IT OUT.
FIGURED WHAT OUT?
OOKAWA-SENPAI. HE'S A RESPECTABLE PERSON ONLY WHEN HE HAS A JOB!
OOKAWA-SENPAI!
YUP?

WILL YOU BE...
...MY COMPANY'S PRESIDENT?
IDIOT! IF I BECOME A COMPANY PRESIDENT, I WON'T BE ABLE TO IDLE MY LIFE AWAY!
I'LL TAKE CARE OF ALL THE HEADACHES.
YOU'D BE REPRESENTATIVE DIRECTOR, AND I'D BE DIRECTOR.
WILL YOU RUN A BUSINESS WITH ME!?

WHAT'S THE SALARY?
SA (SHWIP)
DON'T LOOK AWAY!! THAT'S IMPORTANT!!
LET'S BOTH WORK PART-TIME GIGS TO GET BY UNTIL OUR BUSINESS INCOME STABILIZES...
IT'S YOUR THING. YOU SHOULD BE THE PRESIDENT.
BUT PRESIDENT HAS THE RIGHT TO MAKE FINAL DECISIONS, RIGHT?
I TEND TO LET MY FEELINGS TAKE CONTROL AND GO CHARGING AHEAD. I'D WANT YOU TO KEEP ME IN CHECK WITH AN OBJECTIVE VIEWPOINT.
PLUS, I'LL STILL BE A STUDENT FOR A LITTLE WHILE, AND MINORS CAN'T DO BUSINESS DEALINGS ON THEIR OWN...
AND YOU'RE ALMOST TWENTY, WHICH IS THE AGE OF MAJORITY...

AH! OBVIOUSLY, IF YOU FIND A GOOD JOB ELSEWHERE, I WOULDN'T FORCE YOU TO—
SURE, I'LL DO IT.
YOU WILL !?
I'VE GOT NOTHING BETTER TO DO ANYWAY.
AND HOW COULD I REFUSE A REQUEST FROM MY JUNIOR?
GLAD TO WORK WITH YA...
...VICE PREZ!
YEAH!
THANK YOU VERY MU...
SA (SWHIP)
さっ
すかっ
SUKA (WHIFF)
YOU JERK !!
GYA HA HA HA HA HA HA!
YOU'RE SO GULLIBLE. YOU'RE NOT CUT OUT TO BE A COMPANY PREZ!
YEAH, YEAH !!
I'LL BE THE JERK BOSS, YOU'LL BE THE BOSS WHO'S HONEST TO A FAULT.
OKAY, VICE PREZ !?

...OH!
THIS FEEL-ING...
IT REMINDS ME OF HOW I FELT MY FIRST TIME RIDING!
HEY, YOU'RE RIGHT!
THIS IS GREAT. IT'S LIKE, IT ALL STARTS FROM HERE!
THAT TAKES ME BACK.
I FELL OFF THE HORSE MY FIRST TIME.
UH...
THAT DOESN'T BODE WELL...

Silver Spoon

KEI URYUU

WEST MOSEUSHI
MIDDLE SCHOOL

BASEBALL TEAM
FOURTH BATTER, RIGHT
FIELDER, COLLEGE-BOUND

AGRICULTURAL
ENGINEERING PROGRAM

Chapter 102: Tale of Four Seasons ⑤

HACHI-KEEN.
HURRY UP AND CREATE OUR COMPANYYY.
I'M BORED.
PLEASE WAIT UNTIL MY PROPOSAL GOES THROUGH!
OOKAWA-SAN'S HERE AGAIN?
HE HAS WAY TOO MUCH TIME ON HIS HANDS...
HOW GOES THE PIG FARM?
FINISHED THE REMODEL IN TWO SHAKES OF A LAMB'S TAIL.
ON THE DAYS I CAN'T GO CHECK ON THE PIG, MIKAGE'S GRANDDAD FEEDS HER.
C'MOOON. DON'T YOU HAVE ANYTHING FOR ME TO DO?
GIMME A JOB. PRESIDENT'S ORDERS!
C'MON!
C'MON!
C'MON!
UHHH...

UMMM... OKAY, BUSINESS CARDS. CAN YOU DESIGN SOME FOR US?
I'LL LEAVE THE WHOLE THING TO YOU.
PLEASE DON'T INTERRUPT CLUB.
YOU GOT IT! I CAN TOTALLY DO THAT!
WHAT DO WE DO FOR THE COMPANY NAME?
MMM... SOMETHING LIKE "SILVER SPOON," TO CAPTURE THE IDEA OF NEVER GOING HUNGRY?
GOTCHA. I'LL CHECK WHETHER ANOTHER COMPANY IS ALREADY REGISTERED UNDER THAT NAME AND GO WITH SOMETHING CLOSE.
ZZZ...
GOTTA WORK, GOTTA WORK. ♪
THANKS IN ADVANCE!
THAT SHOULD KEEP HIM OUT OF MY HAIR FOR A LITTLE WHILE...
CAW! CAW!
THE BUSINESS CARD DESIGNS ARE DONE!
I GOT THEM PRINTED!
SHU (SHWIP)
YOU WORK TOO FAST!!!

I MADE PERSONAL ONES FOR YOU WHILE I WAS AT IT!
WOW, THAT'S AMAZING! THANKS SO M...
ぴら
PIRA (FLIP)
KYOO-HOO-HOOT!
SILVER SPOON
HEH-HEH...
DIDN'T EVEN HAVE TO ASK NISHIKAWA. I CAN DRAW THAT STUFF NOW.
I SYMPATHIZE. BUT PLEASE, DON'T!!
OOKAWA-SAN'S AS HANDY AND QUICK A WORKER AS EVER.
WITH HACHIKEN-SENPAI'S SERIOUS SIDE AND OOKAWA-SAN'S HANDINESS COMBINED, COULDN'T THIS TURN OUT TO BE A PRETTY GOOD COMPANY...?
YOU SAID IT.
I BET THERE ARE PEOPLE WHO'D INVEST IN THEM.
YOU CAN DO IT, GUYS!
THAT'S WHAT YOU MIGHT THINK, RIGHT? BUT—

1.
A STAFF OF TWO MINORS.
2.
UNCLEAR BUSINESS HOURS.
3.
STILL LOOKING FOR INVES-TORS.
NO GO.
4.
THEIR CURRENT ASSETS ARE ONE PIG AND ONE LAPTOP.
5.
THEY HAVE BUSINESS CARDS, BUT EXIST ONLY IN NAME.
6.
THEIR DIRECTOR ONCE RAN A FUND.
Ooeze Agricultural High School Eat Pork Club
WE MADE THIS

LAST BUT NOT LEAST ...
7. HE'S THE COMPANY PRESIDENT.
WHAT DO YOU THINK?
SEEMS SHADY...
I HEARD THAT SECOND-YEAR HACHIKEN MADE A DUMMY CORPORATION AND IS LOOKING FOR INVESTORS.
MRMR
WHAT THE HECK? THAT'S SO SHADY!
MRMR
A CON MAN IN HIS SECOND YEAR OF HIGH SCHOOL ...
MRMR
ISN'T HE THAT SMART KID?

EZO
11
BETTER NOT LET HIM TRICK US!
I HAVE A DEAL WITH MY DAD TO INVEST IN ME!! THAT'S IT!!
HACHI-KEN'S DAD?
MRMR
ISN'T HE THAT GUY WHO LOOKS LIKE HE BELONGS IN THE YAK●ZA...?
Y'KNOW THAT SECOND-YEAR, HACHI-KEN?
PEOPLE ARE SAYING HE'S GETTING A LOAN FROM THE YA●UZA TO START A BUSINESS.
SCARY!
AUER
WOW, REALLY...? THAT SCARY-LOOKING DUDE...
INVEST-MENT...
A MAN WHO LOOKS LIKE A Y●KUZA...
AIM FOR THE CHAMPIONSHIPS!!
NO!!
I MEAN, YES, HE HAS THE FACE OF AN ASSASSIN!!
BUT HE'S NOT A GANG-STER!!!
THE FACE OF A MUR-DERER?
MRMR

HACHIKEN, YOU'RE GONNA GET A LOAN FROM A YAK●ZA HITMAN?
IS IT TRUE THEY'LL SELL YOUR ORGANS IF YOUR BUSINESS FAILS?
YOUR STOCK PRICE CRASHED BEFORE YOU EVEN STARTED THE BUSINESS.
HOLD
NNNGH...!!
OOKAWA-SAN, ARE YOU SURE YOU AREN'T A GOD OF DISASTER?
A GOD OF DISASTER IS STILL A GOD.
"WHEN GOD SHUTS ONE DOOR, HE OPENS ANOTHER."
IF YOU END UP UNEMPLOYED, YODA, I AIN'T GONNA HIRE YOU.
2012 7 JULY
YOU COULDN'T PAY ME TO WORK FOR YOU!!
PLUS, I'M TAKING OVER THE FAMILY BUSINESS. I ALREADY HAVE A JOB!!

2012 7 JULY
YOU'LL BE RETIRING FROM CLUB AFTER OUR NEXT MEET, RIGHT, YODA-SENPAI? TIME SURE FLIES.
OH YEAH ...
IF WE WIN AND ADVANCE TO THE NEXT ROUND, I'LL HAVE MORE MEETS!!
ble duty
change
→ Kino
...HE'S RIGHT, THOUGH ...
IT'S TIME I STARTED THINKING ABOUT HANDING OFF THE REINS...
The Pre-farmer's Buddy
How Money-Making Men Start Businesses
HOW TO
HACHI-KEN.
AH, YES!

I WANT TO CONSULT WITH YOU ABOUT OUR CLUB'S FUTURE LEADERSHIP.
EH?
YOU WANT ME TO BE THE NEXT CLUB PRESIDENT!?
YEAH.
WAIT. WAIT. WAIT. SHOULDN'T IT BE HACHIKEN-KUN!?
HE AND I TALKED IT OUT AND DECIDED IT SHOULD BE YOU.

WE ALREADY GOT THE OKAY FROM THE OTHERS TOO.
If that means we won't get stuck with boring jobs...
Agreed!!
DON'T DECIDE EVERYTHING BEHIND MY BACK! THAT'S NOT FAIR!!
WELL, IF YOU WERE STILL THE OLD YOU, I MIGHT NOT HAVE FELT COMFORTABLE ENTRUSTING THE POSITION TO YOU.
FIRST OF ALL, YOU'RE THE BEST WITH HORSES IN THE CLUB.
PLUS, YOU'VE BEEN MORE PROACTIVE ABOUT THINGS SINCE AROUND THE TIME OF EZO AG FEST, RIGHT?
DAIRY SCIENCE 2-D
THE CLUB VALUES THAT.
AS YOU ARE NOW, I CAN COUNT ON YOU TO TAKE THE REINS AS CLUB PRESIDENT.

ERR...BUT I'M SO DUMB I NEED TO FOCUS ON MY STUDIES FOR GETTING INTO COLLEGE...
DAIRY SCIENCE 2-D
GARA (SLIDE)
HAVING EXPERIENCE AS EQUESTRIAN CLUB PRESIDENT ON YOUR OOEZO U RECOMMENDATION APPLICATION WILL WORK TO YOUR ADVANTAGE.
DO IT ALL. JUMP ON ANY EXPERIENCE YOU COULD WEAPONIZE FOR YOUR INTERVIEW OR ESSAY.
USE EVERYTHING YOU'VE GOT TO BUILD YOUR STRATEGY AND CLINCH THAT RECOMMENDATION.
EHHHHHH!?
AS FOR ME, WELL... YOU KNOW. ALTHOUGH I'M ONLY IS SO-SO AT RIDING FOR A SENPAI...
...GAH. I'M SAD TO ADMIT IT.
...I WANT TO LEAVE BEHIND THE BEST I CAN FOR MY JUNIORS.
BE CLUB PRESIDENT, MIKAGE.
BUILD UP YOUR EXPERIENCE AND WEAPONIZE IT.

...I'LL DO IT!
GOOD!
THIS IS A PART OF YOUR COLLEGE PREP TOO. AS CLUB VICE PREZ, I'LL SUPPORT YOU WITH EVERYTHING I'VE GOT!
NNNGH... THANKS...
BUT AM I REALLY GOOD ENOUGH ...?
YOU AND YOUR MOM BOTH TOLD ME, "DON'T PUT YOURSELF DOWN LIKE THAT"!
DO US PROUD, FUTURE PREZ.
AIM FOR KOSHIEN.
DON'T PRESSURE ME!! I'M AWFUL WITH PRESSURE !!
IS THERE A KOSHIEN OF HORSE RIDING?
WOULDN'T IT BE GOTEMBA?
THE INTER-HIGH SCHOOL TOURNAMENT?
MIKAGE, TAKE US TO GOTEMBA!
GET THERE YOUR-SELVES !!
IDIOT! DO YOU THINK WE'RE CAPABLE OF THAT!?

SIGH
SFX: BOBOBUBE (PUTTER)
HEYA.
OH, ICCHAN.
HOW ARE YOU?
GOOD. I GOT THE PAPERWORK FOR THE FIELD RENTAL HERE.
HOW 'BOUT YOU?
YOU LOOK TIRED.
GIVE THIS TO YOUR POPS FOR ME.
OH, A COMMITMENT I WANT TO RUN AWAY FROM CROPPED UP...
BUT I HAVE TO TRY EVERY-THING.
HAAH!
?

DID YER FAMILY START KEEPIN' PIGS?
WE'RE ONLY LETTING OUT THE LAND.
IT'S HACHIKEN-KUN'S BUSINESS'S PIG.
GRNT!
SNRT!
...THAT SAID, IT'S NOT AN OFFICIAL BUSINESS YET.
GRNT!
SNRT!
THEY SAY OOKAWA-SENPAI IS COMPANY PRESIDENT, AND HACHIKEN-KUN IS VICE PRESIDENT.
HACHIKEN AIN'T PRESIDENT?
OOKAWA-SAN IS? WHAT'S GOIN' ON WITH THAT?
OOKAWA-SENPAI NEVER FOUND GAINFUL EMPLOYMENT.
......SO HACHIKEN ADOPTED 'IM? HE AIN'T A STRAY DOG!
HE'S STILL THE SAME SOFTIE WE KNOW.
HE'S GOIN' IN A DIRECTION I'D NEVER HAVE PREDICTED.
HE REALLY IS.
JUST A YEAR AGO, HIS LIFE HAD NOTHING TO DO WITH FARMING, AND LOOK AT HIM NOW!

...STEPPIN' INTO ONE UNKNOWN AFTER ANOTHER LIKE THAT... AIN'T HE SCARED?
HEY, ICCHAN.
YEAH?
WHAT DO YOU THINK IS ON THE OTHER SIDE OF THAT MOUNTAIN?
...MORE MOUN-TAINS?
WHEN I WAS LITTLE, I WAS SURE THERE'D BE A BIG CITY ON THE OTHER SIDE OF THAT MOUNTAIN!
ALL SPARKLY AND SHINY! WITH AN AMUSE-MENT PARK!
SO ONE DAY, CLUTCHING MY POCKET MONEY TIGHT, I CLIMBED UP TO THE SUMMIT ALL BY MYSELF.
OF COURSE, ON THE OTHER SIDE OF THAT MOUNTAIN WAS ONLY THE NEXT MOUNTAIN. I WENT HOME DISAPPOINTED AND GOT A STERN SCOLDING FROM MY FOLKS.

SO THE NEXT TIME I CLIMBED THAT MOUNTAIN, AND GOT DISAPPOINTED WHEN THERE WAS ANOTHER MOUNTAIN BEYOND IT TOO.
AND THAT ONE.
AND THAT ONE.
AND THAT ONE OVER THERE TOO.
AFTER THAT, I CLIMBED THAT MOUNTAIN OVER THERE...
AS I KEPT UP THE CYCLE, CLIMBING AND ENDING UP DISAPPOINTED, I STARTED THINKING THERE'D PROBABLY BE NOTHING ON THE OTHER SIDE OF ANY OF THE MOUNTAINS...
...AND AT SOME POINT, I STOPPED CHECKING WHAT WAS ON THE OTHER SIDE FOR MYSELF WITH MY OWN TWO EYES.
DUMBASS. ALL YOU HAD TO DO WAS CHECK A MAP.
YES, I'M DUMB! I KNOW!

WHEN I WAS A LITTLE KID, I THOUGHT THERE'D BE ANOTHER COUNTRY ON THE OTHER SIDE OF OUR MOUNTAIN RANGE.
WHAT THE HECK!? YOU'RE DUMBER THAN ME!
CALL IT HAVIN' A DREAM!
SFX: BUBOBOBOBO (PUTTER)
AH HA HA!
WHY DON'T YOU TRY CLIMBING A MOUN-TAIN?
YOU JUST MIGHT SEE ANOTHER COUNTRY.

Silver Spoon

FORMER PREZ
BERKSHIRE PIG

Chapter 103
Tale of Four Seasons⑥

OUR COMPANY IS FACING ITS BIGGEST CRISIS SINCE ITS FOUNDATION.
......UH, IT STILL HASN'T BEEN FOUNDED ...
WITH THESE RUMORS GOIN' AROUND THAT WE'RE A DUMMY COMPANY CONNECTED TO THE Y●KUZA, NO ONE WILL INVEST IN US.
RIGHT, BUT I'M GOING TO WRESTLE THE CAPITAL FROM MY DAD SOMEHOW...
YEAH, WELL, WE CAN'T GET ANY MONEY, BECAUSE YOUR POPS, WHO WON'T COUGH UP ANY CASH, LOOKS LIKE A YAK●ZA!!
I'M SORRY MY FATHER HAS CAUSED SO MUCH TROUBLE !!!

I'M SICK AND TIRED OF YOUR PATIENCE!
WE'RE STARTING THIS COMPANY NOW!
EHHH!? BUT HOW ARE WE GOING TO GET ENOUGH MONEY TO KEEP A LOT OF PIGS!?
LOOK. IT'S OOKAWA-SAN.
IT'S THE SHADY PRESIDENT OF THAT SHADY COMPANY.
HOW AWFUL!
I HAVE SAVINGS IN THIS ACCOUNT.
OOEZO BANK
BANK
SHINEI OOKAWA-SAMA
I'LL SINK THIS INTO THE COMPANY, GET US MORE PIGS ASAP, AND SELL, SELL, SELL!!
SO YOU'D HAVE A 100% STAKE OF THE COMPANY?
WHAT ARE YOU TALKING ABOUT? YOU GOTTA COUGH UP THE MONEY TOO!
WE'LL GO HALVES ON THE SHARES!
BUT I'M FLAT BROKE!!
SCHOOL PRECEPTS: WORK, COLLABORATE, DEFY LOGIC
校訓 勤労 協同 理不尽
IF YOU HAVE NO MONEY, THEN MAKE SOME!!
PRESIDENT'S ORDERS! WORK PART-TIME!!
WHAAAAT!?

LISTEN. I GO TO LOTS OF DIFFERENT PLACES FOR PART-TIME GIGS...
...AND EVERYWHERE I GO, WHEN I TALK ABOUT OUR PASTURE-RAISED PIGS, TONS OF PEOPLE SAY THEY WANT TO TASTE THEM EVEN THOUGH THEY WON'T INVEST.
YOU'VE EXPERIENCED IT PLENTY YOURSELF, RIGHT?
PEOPLE BEING WON OVER THROUGH THEIR STOMACHS!
DON'T COUNT ON SOMEBODY ELSE'S MONEY TO START A BUSINESS!!
FIRST, IN THE SCOPE OF YOUR PERSONAL RESPON-SIBILITY, SELL PIGS!!
WHEN WE'VE CAUGHT A WAVE, TAKE THE BUSINESS CARDS, THE MEAT, AND THE BUSINESS RECORDS, AND GO PITCH US TO YOUR POPS!!
AND BAG THAT INVEST-MENT!!
YOU NEED TO HAVE IT OUT WITH HIM WITH FULL CONFIDENCE, NOT AS HIS SON, BUT AS A FULL-FLEDGED WORKING ADULT!!

...WITH MY YAK●ZA-LIKE DAD...?
HE'S NOT GONNA WHACK YOU!
UHHH...IF WE'RE GOING TO KEEP MORE PIGS, WE'LL NEED TO NOTIFY THE LIVESTOCK HEALTH AND SANITATION OFFICE...
ALREADY DID IT.
I TOOK CARE OF THE DISEASE PREVENTION ASSOCIATION REQUIREMENTS TOO.
AL-READY!?
KNOWING YOU, I FIGURED YOU'D WANT TO DO THE DISEASE CONTROL-RELATED STUFF RIGHT.
...I HAD NO IDEA YOU'D BE SUCH A PASSIONATE COMPANY PRESIDENT FOR ME...
HEH HEH...
MAKES ME A HAPPY GUY...!!
WHEN I TOLD MY FAMILY AND RELATIVES I'M BECOMING A COMPANY PRESIDENT, THEY LOOKED AT ME LIKE, "IN YOUR DREAMS, LOSER." I WANT TO MAKE SOME MONEY AND SHOVE IT IN THEIR FACES AS SOON AS POSSIBLE. THAT'S ALL!
OH. I SEE.

Chapter 103: Tale of Four Seasons ⑥

CRAP. THIS IS GONNA BE A REPEAT OF LAST YEAR'S SCHOOL FESTIVAL...
SINCE I DON'T HAVE MORNING AND EVENING CHORES ANYMORE, I GUESS I'LL FILL THE TIME WITH PART-TIME WORK...
WAIT, BUT I HAVE CLUB TOO, AND WE'RE PROBABLY GONNA DO THE HUMAN SLED TEAM EVENT AGAIN FOR THIS YEAR'S FEST...
WORKING 24/7...? IT'S ALREADY STARTING TO SEEM LIKE A SHADY, EXPLOITATIVE COMPANY!!
HEY, IT'S DOABLE. COMPARED TO BEING A FARMER, IT'S TOTALLY DOABLE.
...WHEN YOU KEEP FARM ANIMALS, ARE YOU NOT ABLE TO GO ON FAMILY TRIPS AND STUFF SINCE SOMEBODY ALWAYS HAS TO TAKE CARE OF THE ANIMALS?
THERE ARE DAIRY FARM-HANDS, SO IT CAN BE DONE.

DAIRY FARM-HANDS ...?
YEAH. THEY'RE PROFES-SIONAL HELPERS WHO TAKE CARE OF THE COWS FOR DAIRY FARMERS WHEN THEY'RE AWAY.
IF YOU'RE SIGNED UP WITH A FARMHAND ASSOCIATION OR SOME SIMILAR GROUP, THEY'LL COME HELP OUT.
WE'RE A MEMBER OF ONE TOO, SO WE USE THEIR SERVICE SOMETIMES.
...IT SOUNDS LIKE EVEN DAIRY FARMERS COULD TAKE VACATION IF THEY MADE GOOD USE OF THAT.
HUH?
THEN LAST YEAR, SHOULDN'T YOU HAVE USED THE PROFESSIONAL FARMHANDS INSTEAD OF HAVING ME WORK PART-TIME?
WELL...THE FEES ARE PRETTY HIGH, SO...
IT'S CHEAPER TO HIRE A TEMPO-RARY PART-TIMER.
THAT SAID, YOU CAN'T JUST ASK THEM TO LOWER THE FARMHAND FEES BECAUSE THE ORGANIZATIONS HAVE THEIR OWN OPERATIONAL COSTS.
IF THEY MADE IT TOO CHEAP AND THE ORGANIZATIONS WENT OUT OF BUSINESS, FARMERS WOULDN'T BE ABLE TO USE THEM ANYMORE EITHER. THEN NOBODY WINS.

The Tale of Ichirou Komaba

I EXPECTED IT TO BE TOUGH GIVEN MY AGE, BUT I GUESS MY DAIRY FARM EXPERIENCE AND LARGE VEHICLE LICENSE WERE A PLUS.
NOW WE'LL HAVE A STABLE INCOME FOR A LITTLE WHILE.
ALL RIGHT!!
I CAN REPAY THE MIKAGES LITTLE BY LITTLE...
...AND IF I CAN JUST SELL THE LAND, I'LL BE ABLE TO SEND BOTH NINO AND MISORA OFF TO COLLEGE.
KUMAUSHI DAIRY FARMHANDS ASSOCIATION
WE'RE GETTING SCHOLARSHIP MONEY!!
I KNOW, I KNOW. THAT'S A BIG HELP.
...SO.
WHAT WILL YOU DO NOW?

WILL YOU FINISH HIGH SCHOOL?
ME...?
I AIN'T BOTHERED 'BOUT SCHOOL ANYMORE.
I'LL STAY LOCAL, HELP REPAY OUR DEBT...
NEVER YOU MIND THE DEBT!
I'M ASKING WHAT YOU, PERSONALLY, WANT TO DO.
BUT UNLESS I WORK, THIS FAMILY'LL BE IN TROUBLE.
DON'T FLATTER YOURSELF!
HOW MANY YEARS DO YOU THINK I MANAGED THIS HOUSEHOLD, YOU BIG EATER!?
WHAT DO YOU MOST WANT TO DO!?
SAY IT!

......I WANT MY OWN RANCH.
OKAY. THEN YOU GO FULL SPEED AHEAD CHASING THAT DREAM.
EASIER SAID THAN DONE! EVEN IF I KEEP WORKIN' LIKE I AM, I CAN'T SAVE UP ANY MONEY!
YEAH. THERE AREN'T MANY GOOD-PAYING JOBS HERE.
RIGHT?
THERE'S NOTHIN' I CAN DO ABOUT IT...I DON'T GOT FARMLAND TO INHERIT, I DON'T GOT BASEBALL, I DON'T GOT MONEY. I TRULY HAVE NOTHING NOW...
DO YOU?
DO YOU REALLY HAVE NOTH-ING?

DON'T SPOUT OFF THAT B.S. SO EASILY WHEN THE TRUTH IS, DEEP DOWN, YOU'RE PISSED AS HELL!!!
WHY DON'T YOU TRY CLIMBING A MOUNTAIN?
HERE I HAD YOU PEGGED AS THE TYPE TO USE HIS OWN BRUTE STRENGTH TO WRESTLE DOWN EVEN "LOGIC"...
Restoring Wildland & Adding Value to ...lled Cows Via Hoof Cultivation
HOW DISAP-POINTING.
YOU WORKED ALL DAY LONG AND NOW YOU'RE GONNA PRACTICE BASEBALL!? I STAND BY IT— YOU GUYS ARE CRAZY!!
...MY MUSCLE ...
HUH?

MAYBE I'LL SEE...
...WHAT'S ON THE OTHER SIDE OF THE MOUN-TAINS...
TOKACHI OBIHIRO AIRPORT

It's the final game in the North Hokkaido block of the summer championships, Asahiyama South versus Ooezo Agricultural.
It's the bottom of the ninth and the score is three-two with Asahiyama South in the lead.
ROYCE'
Ooezo Agricultural is chasing that one run...
—And they make a sacrifice bunt! It succeeds! They're at one out with runners on second and third base!
OHH!
PON (BÔNG)
Flight 1154 bound for Haneda...
...will now begin boarding.
OH, TIME TO GO.
SHOOT. IT WAS JUST GETTING GOOD!
HOLD ON, GOTTA SEE THIS BEFORE WE GO.
THIS IS THEIR CHANCE TO TURN IT AROUND...
KIIN (CLANG)
AH!!
A pop up to the catcher... He's out!
That makes two outs!
ARRGH!!

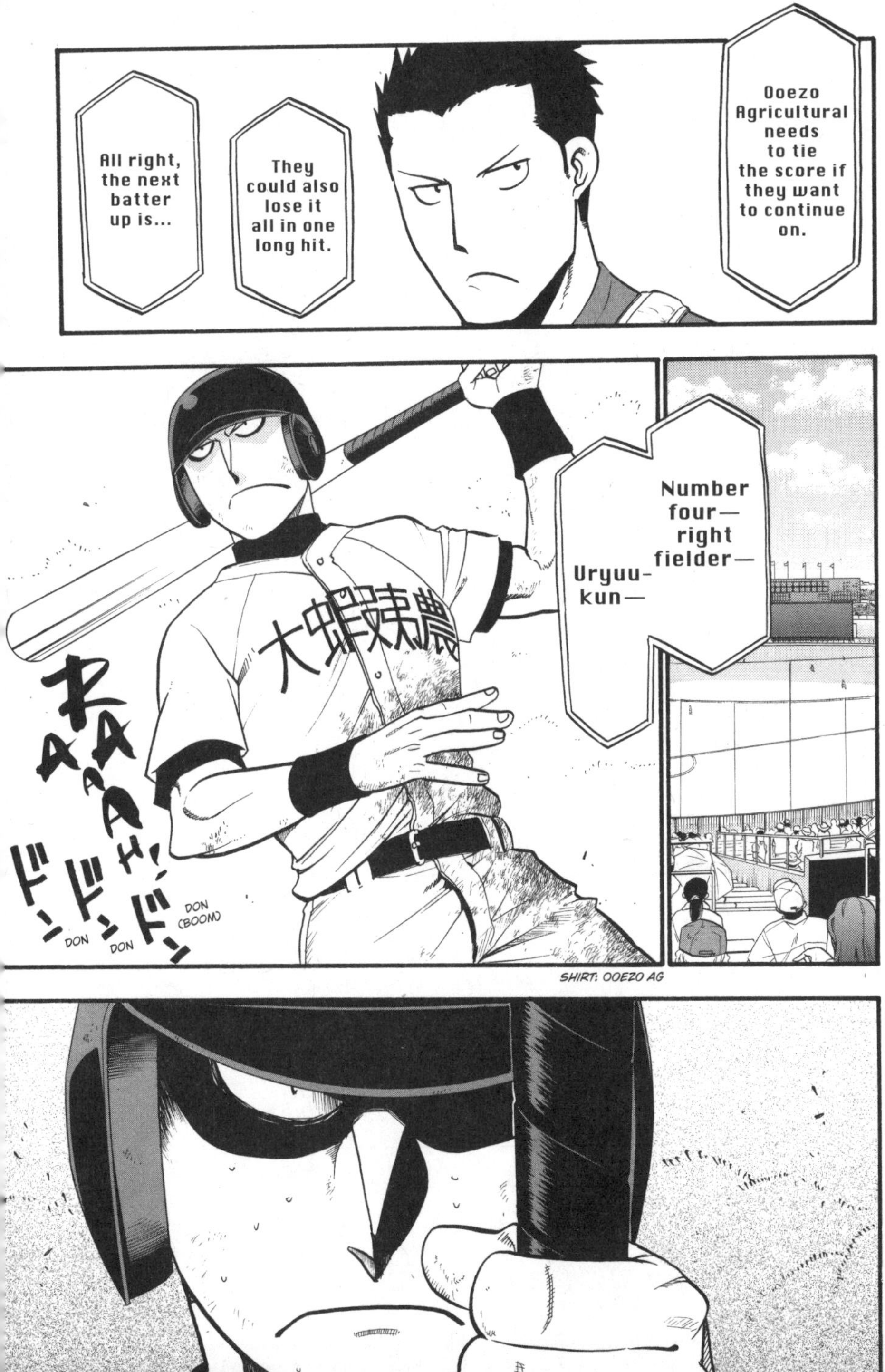
Ooezo Agricultural needs to tie the score if they want to continue on.
They could also lose it all in one long hit.
All right, the next batter up is...
Number four—right fielder—
Uryuu-kun—
RAAAAH!
ドンドンドーン
DON DON DON (BOOM)
SHIRT: OOEZO AG

Here comes the first pitch—
Outside. It's a ball!
Pitch two!
—Oh, it's a foul!
Ball!
Foul!
Foul! A foul again!
Pitch six—ball!
We're on the edge of our seats!

Next—another foul!
They're really keeping us in suspense, folks!
We're at three balls and two strikes, and here comes—
Another foul!
This has turned into quite the battle!
Will Asahi-yama South get away clean!?
Or will Ezo Ag grab their first ticket to Koshien!?

KIIN (CLANG)
It's a hit!!
It's a big one !!!
KII (SQUEAK)
And that white ball goes soaring into the blue sky with all of Ezo Ag's dreams riding on it—
RAAAAAAAH!

Silver Spoon

NINO KOMABA

MISORA KOMABA

ICHIROU KOMABA'S LITTLE SISTERS
TWINS

Chapter 104
Tale of Four Seasons⑦
WHAT SHOULD WE DO FOR THE BRAND NAME OF OUR PASTURE-RAISED PIGS?
SOMETHING TASTY-SOUNDING AND COOL...
A NAME THAT STRIKES A FAMILIAR CHORD...
UMAGOHAN
"EZO PORK"?
"SILVER PORK"?
"SILVER PIG"?
SENPAI IS HERE AGAIN.
WE'RE KEEPING THEM AT MIKAGE'S PLACE, SO "MIKAGE PIG"?
THAT MAKES IT SOUND LIKE I'M A PIG!!

BAG: HORSE FOOD

PIGS HAVE A REALLY LOW BODY FAT PER-CENTAGE, RIGHT?
LIKE MIKAGE STONE, THAT GRANITE FROM MIKAGE, KOBE. COOL, RIGHT?
ALL RIGHT! AS A SALUTE TO THE MIKAGE FAMILY FOR LENDING OUR BUSINESS THE LAND, WE'LL CALL THEM THE "MIKAGE PIG!"
AHHHH!!!
...I'LL INVEST TOO, BECOME THE BIGGEST STAKE-HOLDER, AND CHANGE THE NAME!!!
ALL RIGHT. BAGGED OURSELVES ONE FUTURE INVESTOR.

Chapter 104:

Tale of Four Seasons ⑦

THE FARM WE'RE ABOUT TO VISIT KEEPS 800 PIGS PASTURED IN THE MOUNTAINS.
THIS SAYS THEY KEEP THEM LONGER THAN THE AVERAGE FARM. THEY SHIP THEM OUT ONCE THEY'VE REACHED A WEIGHT OF 170 TO 180 KILOGRAMS.
EIGHT HUNDRED PIGS, AT THAT HUGE SIZE? SOUNDS LIKE A LOT OF WORK.

バン
BAN (SLAM)
バタン
BATAN
HEY, INADA!
LONG TIME NO SEE!
YOU LOOK GOOD, PREZ.
INADA-SENPAI, IT'S GOOD TO SEE YOU!
HELLO!
HEY.
HOW'S YOUR BUSINESS?
......
......
?
SAY SOMETHING!

A FRIEND FROM COLLEGE SET ME UP WITH A SEASONAL JOB HERE FOR SUMMER VACATION.
DISEASE PREVENTION COVERALLS
SIZE L
WE SHOULD GREET THE BOSS.
NOT HERE TODAY.
SAID TO SHOW YOU AROUND, WHEREVER YOU WANT.
WHERE ARE THE OTHER WORKERS?
IT'S ONLY ME TODAY.
GENERALLY SPEAKING, ONE OR TWO PEOPLE IS PLENTY.
HUH...? BUT TO TAKE CARE OF 800 PIGS......
UHHH... HOW BIG IS THIS FARM EXACTLY...?

IT GOES FROM OVER THERE...
...TO ALL THE WAY OVER THERE.
I DON'T KNOW THE EXACT AREA.
......
GRNT!
SQUEE!
OINK!
THEY'RE SO CUTE!!
BEFORE WE RELEASE THEM OUTSIDE, WE KEEP THE PIGLETS IN SAFE PLACES LIKE THIS UNTIL THEY'RE A GOOD SIZE.
PIG GRADE SCHOOL !!
SNRT!
GRNT!

MAY I TOUCH THEM?
SURE THING. THEIR CANINES AREN'T CUT, THOUGH, SO BE CAREFUL.
SNRT!
GRNT!
WEE!
PIG CANINES... LIKE A WILD BOAR'S TUSKS?
YEAH.
RANCHES THAT KEEP LARGE NUMBERS OF PIGS IN A SMALL SPACE WILL CLIP THEIR CANINES AND TAILS SOON AFTER THEY'RE BORN TO PREVENT INJURIES.
KEEPING ANIMALS IN CROWDED SPACES CAUSES STRESS AND LEADS TO MORE FIGHTS. THEIR TAILS WILL GET BITTEN OFF, THINGS LIKE THAT.
BUT THESE GUYS HERE HAVE BARELY ANY STRESS, SO IT'S NOT NECESSARY.
SO YOU SAVE THE TIME AND EFFORT IT'D TAKE TO CLIP THEIR CANINES AND TAILS. THAT SOUNDS NICE.
IF THEY'RE LESS LIKELY TO GET INJURED, YOU CAN GET AWAY WITHOUT USING AS MANY ANTIBIOTICS, SO YOU CAN SAVE COSTS ON THAT END TOO.
AH, BUT THIS RANCH SHIPS THEIR PIGS OUT AT A HIGHER WEIGHT THAN AVERAGE, RIGHT?
IF THE REARING PERIOD IS THAT MUCH LONGER, IT'LL ADD MORE FEED COST TOO. DO THEY NOT MAKE AS MUCH PROFIT?
THIS RANCH MAKES SAUSAGE, BACON, AND OTHER PRODUCTS AT THEIR OWN PROCESSING FACILITY, AND THEY HAVE A LOYAL CUSTOMER BASE, SO THEY MAKE A DECENT PROFIT.

MAKES SENSE. JUST THE WORDS "PASTURE-RAISED PORK" MAKES IT SOUND TASTY.
IT MAKES YOU WANT TO TRY SOME EVEN IF IT'S A LITTLE ON THE PRICEY SIDE.
HUH ...?
COME TO THINK OF IT, I DON'T ACTUALLY SEE ANY OF THE PASTURED PIGS......
USE THESE.
?

!!?
I SEE THEM!! IF YOU LOOK CLOSELY, THEY'RE ALL OVER THE PLACE!!
THEY'RE BLENDING WITH THE COLOR OF THE DIRT!!
ARE THEY DUG INTO THE DIRT FOR AN AFTER-NOON NAP?
THE PINK PIGS LOOK LIKE BLACK PIGS!
APPARENTLY THE SLAUGH-TERHOUSE COMPLAINS THAT THEY'RE TOO DIRTY.

OH, IT'S EATING BAMBOO GRASS.
THEY EAT DIRT, AND THEY GET MINERALS AND FIBER FROM WHATEVER PLANTS GROW HERE.
MAKES THEIR IMMUNE SYSTEMS STRONGER.
THEY'RE GETTING HIGH-CALORIE FEED TOO.
THESE PIGS REALLY ARE LIVING HOWEVER THEY WANT.
EEEK!
ぶるぶるぶる
BURU BURU (SHAKE) BURU
PLAYING IN THE MUD LOOKS LIKE IT FEELS GOOD.
WE LEAVE THEIR EXCREMENT AS FERTILIZER FOR THE SOIL. ALL WE HAVE TO DO IS CHECK A FEW PLACES LIKE THEIR WATER AND THEIR FEED.
HELPERS COME WHEN IT'S TIME TO MOVE THE PIGS OR TO SHIP THEM OUT, BUT ON AN AVERAGE DAY YOU CAN TAKE CARE OF THEM WITH VERY FEW PEOPLE—THAT'S ONE OF THE CHARMS OF PASTURE-RAISED PIG FARMING.
IF I WERE REINCARNATED AS A PORK PIG, I'D WANT TO BELONG TO THIS RANCH.
DON'T FORGET YOU'D HAVE YOUR BALLS REMOVED RIGHT AFTER YOU WERE BORN.
YOU'D BE SINGLE FOR LIFE.
*TALE OF SPRING 7

THIS STYLE OF FARMING SEEMS NICE FROM AN ANIMAL WELFARE POINT OF VIEW TOO.
YEAH.
THE MINIMAL LABOR COSTS ARE APPEALING FROM THE FINANCIAL SIDE AS WELL.
THIS PLACE IS REALLY NICE.
EVERY-BODY SHOULD DO THIS.
PUT SIMPLY, THIS METHOD IS ULTIMATELY BASED ON AVAILABILITY OF LARGE SWATHS OF LAND.
YOU CAN'T DO IT JUST ANY-WHERE.
PLUS, PIGS LOVE TO ROOT, RIGHT?
THEY TEAR UP THE TURF LIKE THIS, SO YOU HAVE TO PREP SEVERAL AREAS OF OPEN LAND AND ROTATE THROUGH THEM.
OH, IT'S TRUE. THE TURF COMES UP REALLY EASILY.
WHEN THIS BATCH IS ALL SHIPPED OUT, THEY'LL HAVE TO LET THIS PARTICULAR PASTURE REST FOR A LITTLE WHILE.
THE NEXT BATCH WILL USE THAT HILL OVER THERE, MAYBE.

SO CO-EXISTING WITH NATURE ISN'T SO EASY, EVEN WITH THIS MUCH LAND...
AGRICULTURE IS BASICALLY THE BUSINESS OF PACKING IN ANIMALS AND PLANTS THAT ARE USEFUL TO HUMANS AT UNNATURAL DENSITIES.
IT'S A DESTRUCTION OF NATURE.
HMMM... I'M DOING AN ANIMAL WELFARE PROJECT. DESTRUCTION OF NATURE IS WORRYING...
HA-HA-HA-HA! WORRY IT UP!
FORMER PREZ... BERKSHIRES DIG INTO THE SOIL LIKE CRAZY, RIGHT?
CRAP. WHEN WE GET MORE PIGS, THE MIKAGES' LAND WILL GO BALD IN NO TIME FLAT.
SPEAKING OF, A NEW BREED THAT DOESN'T ROOT MUCH IS JUST NOW BEING SOLD.
WHAT IS IT!? TELL US ALL ABOUT IT!!
PIG BREEDING IS AMAZING!!
THINK WE'LL BE ABLE TO SHIP OUT OUR BUSINESS'S FIRST PIGS NEXT YEAR?

OUR FIRST SHIPMENT! WHAT SHOULD WE EAT? HOW SHOULD WE SELL IT?
OUR FIRST SHIP-MENT...
I WANT TO TRY SOME-THING.
WHAT IS IT? SAUSAGE? BACON?
I WANT TO MAKE PIZZAS AGAIN.

WHEN I WAS AT MY LOWEST WITH NO CONFIDENCE, PIZZA WAS THE SPARK THAT LED TO ME GETTING BACK UP.
I WANT TO DO IT AGAIN.
WITH EZO AG'S BRICK OVEN? CAN WE BORROW THAT?
PEOPLE ARE DRAWN TO THAT THING LIKE A MAGNET. WE'D END UP WAY IN THE RED.
LET'S SELL THEM THIS TIME AND TURN A PROFIT.
WE GONNA ASK THEM TO LET US SELL IT ON EZO AG'S CAMPUS?
NO...
SIGN: BAN'EI TOKACHI
I HAVE SOMETHING ELSE IN MIND.

BAN'EI CELEBRATION
Ban'ei Tokachi
Ban'ei Tokachi
R
TOKACHI AGRICULTURAL COOPERATIVE
OBIHIRO RACETRACK

FOOD SAFETY
Ban'ei Tokachi
Ban'ei Tokachi

WAGES
achiken-dono
馬術部

WEL-
COME
HOME,
DEAR.
MM.
I'M
HOME.
...YUUGO
HASN'T
SENT ANY
PROPOSALS
RECENTLY.
OH!
NOW
THAT YOU
MENTION
IT, HE
HASN'T.
...WHEN I GO TO
DEPOSIT YUUGO'S
POCKET MONEY,
I CHECK THE
MONTHLY ACCOUNT
BALANCE...
...AND HIS
SAVINGS
ARE
CREEPING
UP
STEADILY
EVERY
MONTH.
BEYOND
JUST THE
POCKET
MONEY.
IT LOOKS
LIKE HE'S
WORKING
HARD AT
PART-TIME
JOBS.

...I SEE.

Silver Spoon

NAMI KOMABA

ICHIROU KOMABA'S
MOTHER

Chapter 105
Tale of Four Seasons⑧

BOTTLE: JINGISU JUICE / SEMI-CARBONATED

GERMAN PIZZA !!!
POTATOES, BACON, AND CHEESE.
THE TASTE CHANGES A LOT DEPENDING ON THE VARIETY.
THE VARIETIES WE GROW THAT COULD GO GOOD WITH YOUR PIZZAS WOULD BE...LET'S SEE...
YOUR FAMILY GROWS POTATOES, RIGHT!?
YEP.
IT'LL BE CHEAP IF YA BUY 'EM DIRECTLY FROM US.
GREAT!!
IRISH COBBLER !!
FIRST GROWN BY IRISH SHOEMAKERS IN AMERICA!!
I'M YER NUMBER ONE GAL!!
ADAPTABLE TO DIFFERENT ENVIRONMENTS, HER HIGH CROP YIELD AND SOFT, FLAKY MOUTHFEEL HAS EARNED HER LOTS OF FANS!!

KITA AKARI!!
COMPARED TO THE IRISH COBBLER, THIS VARIETY'S FLESH IS MORE YELLOW AND BREAKS APART MORE EASILY WHEN BOILED. SHE LOOKS ROUGHER ON THE OUTSIDE TOO, BUT SHE'S A BEAUTY ON THE INSIDE WITH SWEETNESS AND HIGH NUTRITIONAL VALUE!!!
I HAVE... LOTS OF... VITAMIN C!
MAY QUEEN!!
THIS VARIETY ORIGINATED IN ENGLAND!!
IF THEY HAVE NO BREAD...
...THEN LET THEM EAT POTATOES!
SHE DOESN'T CRUMBLE AS EASILY AS IRISH COBBLERS AND HAS A SMOOTHER TEXTURE!! AND SHE'S EASY TO PEEL!!
THE AWAKENING OF INCA!!
D-DON'T THINK JUST CAUSE I'M SMALL...
...YOU CAN MAKE A FOOL OUT OF ME!!
SMALL-SIZED AND SUPER-SWEET!! YOU CAN'T GET ENOUGH OF THE CHESTNUTTY TASTE!!
THE FLESH OF THIS VARIETY IS A DEEP GOLD WITH LOTS OF CAROTENOID PIGMENT, WHICH HAS A STRONG ANTIOXIDANT EFFECT!
SHADOW QUEEN!!
A VIVID PURPLE COLOR!! CONTAINING LOTS OF ANTHOCYANIN, HER POPULARITY IS ON THE RISE AS A HEALTHY FOOD!!
I'LL CAST A MAGIC SPELL...
...OF HEALTH ON YOU!
SHE HAS A CURIOUS TEXTURE BETWEEN REGULAR POTATOES AND SWEET POTATOES!!

NORTHERN RUBY!!
SHE'S ANOTHER VARIETY WITH LOTS OF ANTHOCYANIN. SHE'S A BEAUTIFUL PINK BOTH OUTSIDE AND IN!!
PINK VICHYSSOISE SOUP!
EAT UP! EAT UP! ♡
COMPARED TO THE IRISH COBBLER, SHE HAS A FIRM AND STICKY TEXTURE!!
RED MOON!!
TRUE TO HER NAME, SHE'S A BRIGHT SCARLET ON THE OUTSIDE!!
DON'T THINK FOR A MOMENT...
...YOU CAN MAKE ME YOURS SO EASILY.
SHE'S A RARE POTATO WHO'S DIFFICULT TO STORE AND HAS A LOW QUANTITY ON THE MARKET!!
SHE DOESN'T CRUMBLE WHETHER STEWED OR FRIED, SO SHE MAKES FOR BEAUTIFUL FINISHED DISHES!!
GROUND PECHIKA!!
ORIGINATED AS A VARIANT OF RED MOON!! ALSO KNOWN AS "DESTROYER"!!!
LOOK AT THE REAL ME...
IT'S HARD TO KNOW WHAT TO EXPECT FROM THAT APPEARANCE, BUT ONCE PEELED, SHE'S A BEAUTIFUL GOLDEN COLOR!!
THIS VARIETY'S DEEP BODY WILL HAVE YOU HOOKED!!
TOKACHI KOGANE!!
I TAKE GREAT PRIDE...
...IN MY STEADY CHARACTER.
SOFT YET NOT CRUMBLY!! AND GOOD COLD TOO!! SHE STORES WELL AND HAS HAD A SUDDEN BURST OF POPULARITY IN RECENT YEARS!!
AND SAYAKA, AND HARUKA, AND KOGANEMARU...
WHICH GIRL DO YOU WANT?
YOU REALLY LOVE YOUR POTATOES...

GERMAN PIZZA!?
THAT SOUNDS GREAT!!
LEAVE THE CHEESE TO ME!
Cheese Research Club Today's Activity: Tasting!!
Sales
I WAS PLANNING ON IT.
SHOULD I DO GOUDA OR RACLETTE...?
I WANT TO EXPERIMENT WITH MOZZARELLA TOO!
TRADITIONAL MOZZARELLA IS MADE WITH BUFFALO'S MILK, RIGHT?
BUT THEY SELL MOZZARELLA MADE FROM HOLSTEIN MILK TOO, RIGHT?
THE BUFFALO MOZZARELLA HAS WAY MORE BODY.
PLUS, I'VE HEARD THAT FRESH MOZZARELLA TASTES EXCEPTIONAL.

BUFFALO, THOUGH... SOUNDS LIKE AN ANIMAL THAT WOULD BE KEPT IN THE TROPICS.
LIKE ON ISHIGAKI ISLAND.
ALL RIGHTY!! MAYBE I'LL VISIT ISHIGAKI ISLAND ON THE CHEESE RESEARCH CLUB BUDGET!!
THERE ARE FARMS IN HOKKAIDO THAT KEEP BUFFALO AS WELL!!
YOU HAVE BEEN RACKING UP TOO MANY EXPENSES EVER SINCE YOU BECAME THE CHEESE RESEARCH CLUB'S PRESIDENT!!
IF YOU'RE ALWAYS PINCHING PENNIES, YOU WON'T GET TO EAT THE GOOD STUFF.
TCH!
OKAY, THEN LET'S POWER UP OUR RACLETTE.
IT'S TOO LIGHT WITH ONLY HOLSTEIN MILK, SO LET'S BRING IN JERSEY AND BROWN SWISS MILK TOO.
BROWN SWISS
MORE FAT AND PROTEIN THAN IN HOLSTEIN MILK
JERSEY
MORE FAT IN MILK, RICH IN CAROTENE
DO YOU KNOW HOW MUCH THAT WILL COST!?
BUY THEEEM!! BUY ME COWS!!
PLEASE! PLEASE!
DO NOT ASK LIKE A CHILD BEGGING FOR A TOY!!
SHE'S GOING TO FORCE HIM TO BUY THEM.
UH-HUH.

Chapter 105:

Tale of Four Seasons ⑧

"FOOD SALES PERMIT APPLICATION"......
"FOOD SANITATION SUPERVISOR"... WHAT ELSE... LET'S SEE...
food sales permit application
Gugule
food sales permit application
Web Images Videos News More
MAN, IT'S A HASSLE TO GO THROUGH ALL THE PROCEDURES TO SELL YOUR OWN PIZZA.
EQUESTRIAN CLUB
SHOULD WE SPLIT THE QUALIFICATIONS AND PERMITS AND SO ON BETWEEN YOU AND ME?
NAH, YOU HELP MIKAGE STUDY.
I'LL TAKE CARE OF ALL OF THIS.
OOKAWA SENPAI IS SO NICE!!
SEE!? I MADE THE RIGHT CHOICE! ONCE YOU GIVE HIM A JOB, HE REALLY SHINES!!
PSST! PSST! PSST! PST! PST!
MY POSITION'S SAFE IF I MAKE SURE HE CAN'T SELL ANYTHING WITHOUT ME...
THESE FIRST PIZZA SALES ARE ONLY AN EXPERIMENT, SO IT COULD BE A GOOD IDEA TO JUST TEMPORARILY ROPE IN SOMEONE WHO ALREADY HAS THE QUALIFICATIONS...
...AH.

IF YOUR BRO WANTS TO RUN A RAMEN RESTAURANT, HE MUST HAVE BUSINESS SMARTS, COOKING SMARTS, AND LICENSES, RIGHT?
DON'T.
THE ONLY LICENSE HE HAS IS A LICENSE TO KILL!!
SO MUCH FOR THAT. GUESS I'LL GO GET THE WHOLE SHEBANG OF QUALIFICATIONS MYSELF.
OOKAWA-SENPAI, IF YOU HAVE THAT MANY QUALIFICATIONS, COULDN'T YOU MAKE MORE MONEY AT ANOTHER JOB...?
SHH!!
INTER-HIGH COMPETITION
HOKKAIDO QUALIFIERS
June 8-9
Northern Horse Park
2013
JUNE
OH YEAH. IT'S ALMOST INTER-HIGH SEASON!
-HIGH COMPETITION
KAIDO QUALIFIERS
June 8-9
Northern Horse Park
2013
JUNE
HOW'S IT LOOKING THIS YEAR?
WE GOT A REALLY GOOD FIRST-YEAR!

OH! THAT KID WHO WAS IN THE SAME RIDING CLUB AS MIKAGE! NAME'S, UH...
ISHI-YAMA.
HELLO!
WHO ARE YOU ENTERING IN THE TEAM COMPETI-TION?
MIKAGE AND ISHIYAMA. WE'LL PICK ONE OTHER PERSON FROM AMONG US THIRD-YEARS ONCE WE SEE WHO'S COMPATIBLE WITH THE HORSES AT THE RING.
NO SECOND-YEARS?
SHE'S ...
SHU (SHFF)
SHU
SHU
SHU
SHU

ふき ふき
FUKI
FUKI (WIPE)
ふき ふき
FUKI FUKI
しゅっ しゅっ
SHU SHU
しゅっ しゅっ しゅっ
SHU SHU SHU
YOU'RE GROOMING THEM PRETTY METICU-LOUSLY.
Y...YES, SIR!!
'COS THIS IS THE LAST TIME YOU SENPAIS WILL BE COMPETING AS A GROUP...
AND OUR HORSES WILL BE TROTTING INTO THE SPOTLIGHT TOGETHER TOO, SO...
I WANT EVERYONE TO SEE HOW COOL OUR HORSES ARE...

FOR THIS COMPETITION, WE'LL BE USING HORSES THEY PROVIDE AT THE RING.
LOANED HORSES.
YEAH, WE'RE NOT TAKIN' OUR HORSES.
!!?
...IS SHE ALL THERE?
SHE HAS A LOT OF PASSION AND TENDS TO SPIN HER WHEELS.
BUT THE HORSES ALL LOVE HER BECAUSE SHE TAKES CARE OF THEM SO CAREFULLY.
WE CAN FEEL SAFE ENTRUSTING THE HORSES TO HER.
YEAH.

NORTHERN HORSE PARK
Garden Dining K's Garden
RESTAURANT BARBECUE
CARRIAGE HORSE GALLERY
CLOSED 12/26 1/15
Horse Riding Meet June 8~9
Founding Celebration
SHIRT: HIDAKA AGRICULTURAL EQUESTRIAN CLUB
EZO AG'S CLUB? HELLO.
HELLO, SIR.
HELLO TO THOSE OF YOU FROM HIDAKA AGRICULTURAL.
HELLO THERE!
HIDAKA AGRICULTURE BREEDS THEIR OWN RACEHORSES, RIGHT?
THEIR EQUESTRIAN CLUB IS STRONG TOO.
THEY'RE UP AGAINST US FIRST.
UGH, WE'RE GONNA LOSE!

WHICH HORSES ARE WE RIDING?
LET'S SEE...
IT SAYS CAROL SEVEN, MOMOTAROU, AND AIKO.
MOMOTAROU IS A BIT QUIRKY AND FINNICKY, IF I REMEMBER RIGHT.
AKI, YOU LIKE THE BOTH-ERSOME HORSES, RIGHT?
OH, THEY'RE DOING WARM-UP EXERCISES RIGHT NOW.
THAT'S MOMO-TAROU.
WOW! SO PRETTY ...
KURU (TURN)
......

...I'M STARTING TO FEEL LIKE WE CAN WIN!
YEAH!
WHOA!
WHOA, WHOA, WHOA!!
BRR HRRR!
HEYYY! NOT THAT WAY!!
ズザー
ZUZAAA (SKSHH)
BWEH!
PAKA (CLOP)
ぱか
POKO (KLOP)
ぽこ
ぱか
PAKA
ぽこ
POKO
ぱか
PAKA
...OH?

とこ
TOKO (TROT)
とこ
TOKO
とこ
TOKO
とこ
TOKO
とこ
TOKO
SAKAE KNOWS EXACTLY HOW TO RIDE THAT HORSE.
ZAN (BAM)
NO SUR-PRISES FROM MIKAGE ...
AND ISHI-YAMA ...
OHP, OHP, OHP!
THAT HORSE IS SWEET ON WOMEN!!!
THAT'S DIS-CRIMI-NATION!!!
A FINICKY HORSE? MORE LIKE AN OBVIOUS ONE!!
THAT'S OUR TIME! PRACTICE IS OVER!

I WILL NOW ANNOUNCE THE NAMES OF THE THREE MEMBERS WHO WILL COMPETE IN THE TEAM COMPETITION'S FIRST ROUND.
MI-KAGE-SAN.
YES, SIR.
ISHI-YAMA-KUN.
YES, SIR!
AND THE THIRD WILL BE...
ドッ DO (BADUM)
ドッ DO
ドッ DO
ドッ DO
ドッ DO
ドッ DO
ドッ DO
ドッ DO
ドッ DO

SAKAE-SAN.
ME!?
OH GOSH, OH GOSH! IT'S MY TIME TO SHINE!!
BREAK A LEG!
WE'RE COUNTING ON YOU!
WE'LL RETRIEVE YOUR BODY!
YOU CAN DO IT, SAKAE-SENPAI!!
...I'M DISAPPOINTED I DIDN'T GET CHOSEN...
WHEW...
...BUT AT THE SAME TIME, I'M RELIEVED I DON'T HAVE THAT HEAVY RESPONSIBILITY ON MY SHOULDERS...
WELL, COMPATIBILITY WITH THE HORSE IS IMPORTANT.
NOTHING I CAN DO ABOUT IT...
IF WE ADVANCE TO THE FINALS—HACHIKEN-KUN, I'D LIKE YOU TO COMPETE.
BWUH!?

Silver Spoon 12 • END

Silver Spoon

Eye Power

ギン
GIN
(GLARE)
びくぅ
BIKUU
(JOLT)
ギン
GIN
ばたん
BATAN
(FLOP)
ギン
GIN
ばりっ
BARI
(RIP)

Cow Shed Diaries:
"Finally Being Able to Go See the Movie" Chapter

THE MOVIE PREMIERED ON MARCH 7, BUT BETWEEN WORK AND LIFE I COULDN'T SEEM TO GET TO THE THEATER...
AH!! MOST THEATERS IN KANTO HAVE ALREADY FINISHED SHOWING IT!
MOVIE SCHEDULE
AND SO I SAW THE MOVIE IN MAY WHILE I WAS IN HOKKAIDO FOR RESEARCH.
TO THINK I'D END UP SEEING IT IN THE HOLY LAND...!
Silver Spoo
WHEN WE WENT, ONLY THE VERY FRONT ROW HAD OPEN SEATS, SO WE GOT STUCK CRANING OUR NECKS UP TO SEE THE SCREEN...
MY NECK'S SO TIRED...
BIG SISTERS
THE FRONT ROW IS NUTS...
BUT BECAUSE OF THAT, THE DRAFT HORSE RACE SCENE WAS INCREDIBLY POWERFUL!!!
ZUZUN (BATHOOM)
YOU CAN REALLY FEEL IT! THAT IF YOU GOT STEPPED ON YOU'D DIE!!!
WHOA!

Silver Spoon 12!
Drawing this made me want to keep pigs. Their distance from humans is just right. And they have this perfect laidback feel.

あらかわひろむ
Hiromu Arakawa

~ Special Thanks ~
All of my assistants,
Everyone who helped with collecting material, interviews, and consulting,
My editor, Mr. Tsubouchi, Mr. Yamada

AND YOU!!

NEXT......

They have dreams they want to realize, and friends they want to walk alongside. Their long yet short three years at Ooezo Agricultural High School nurtured something precious that can't be bundled up as mere "memories."

And now, Hachiken, Mikage, Komaba, and all the rest have taken a giant step toward each of their dreams. *Silver Spoon* 13, coming soon!!

to be continued......

Silver
Spoon

HACHI-KEN'S MOM
AMONG THE EZO AG STUDENTS, SHE'S KNOWN AS THE "GANGWIFE."
THE GANGWIFE...
IT'S THE GANGWIFE...
IS SHE HERE TO BUY VEGETABLES?

Translation Notes

Common Honorifics

no honorific: Indicates familiarity or closeness; if used without permission or reason, addressing someone in this manner would constitute an insult.
-san: The Japanese equivalent of Mr./Mrs./Miss. If a situation calls for politeness, this is the fail-safe honorific.
-sama: Conveys great respect; may also indicate the social status of the speaker is lower than that of the addressee.
-kun: Used most often when referring to boys, this honorific indicates affection or familiarity. Occasionally used by older men among their peers, but it may also be used by anyone referring to a person of lower standing.
-chan: An affectionate honorific indicating familiarity used mostly in reference to girls; also used in reference to cute persons or animals of either gender.
-sensei: A respectful term for teachers, artists, or high-level professionals.
-niisan, nii-san, aniki, etc.: A term of endearment meaning "big brother" that may be more widely used to address any young man who is like a brother, regardless of whether he is related or not.
-neesan, nee-san, aneki, etc.: The female counterpart of the above, *neesan* means "big sister."

Currency Conversion

While conversion rates fluctuate, an easy estimate for Japanese yen conversion is ¥100 to 1 USD.

Page 8
The Twelve Level Cap and Rank System: The first of several similar systems employed during this period of Japanese history under which people's court ranks were indicated with caps and feathers.

Japanese missions to Sui China: The sending of diplomatic delegations to be received in the Imperial Court of China.

Taika Reform: The set of reforms marking the end of the Asuka period. The aim of the reforms was to centralize power within the Imperial court. ("*Taika*" means "Great Reform.")

The capital relocates to Nara: The capital of Japan moved several times throughout history before finally becoming Tokyo in 1868. When the city of Nara was the capital, it was officially known as Heijo-kyo.

The Kojiki: The oldest surviving text from Japan. A book of history including Japanese mythology and a genealogy of emperors, compiled by court scholar O no Yasumaro in 712.

The Nihon Shoki: Another chronicle of Japanese history and legends, compiled in 720.

The Konden Einen Shizai Law: Before this law, farmers were only allowed to succeed their land for three generations. With this law, they were able to own their land permanently.

Page 31
Kagoshima Black Pork is the most famous high-end black pork brand in Japan—like the Kobe beef of pork.

Page 39
The Rose of Versailles is a classic manga by prolific manga artist Riyoko Ikeda. Set in historical France around the time of the French Revolution, the story follows Oscar, a girl raised as a man to succeed her father as leader of the palace guards.

Page 47
Kofuku Station is a closed railway station in Obihiro, Hokkaido. Since "*kofuku*" means "happiness," it's a popular sightseeing spot.

Page 48
The Japanese language system has three sets of characters: hiragana, katakana, and kanji. Hiragana and katakana are phonetic, and each character represents a syllable sound. Kanji are more complex characters representing words and concepts. Mikage has attempted to make her essay seem longer than it is by spelling out kanji phonetically, rather than using the single characters, which boosts her total character count.

Page 72
There are three years of high school in Japan, and the National Center Test for University Admissions is administered every January. If Ayame is going to take college entrance exams in her final year of high school, this gives Shingo just a year and a half to whip her into shape.

Page 117
Gotemba is a city in Shizuoka Prefecture near Mount Fuji that is home to a large competition center.

Page 146
Mikage, Kobe is an area of Japan known for its high-quality granite mines. It is so well known, the area's name has become synonymous with granite.

Page 168
Nishikawa's personifications of potato varieties as cute girls is similar to the many mobile and browser games that personify things like warships, weapons, etc., as cute boys or girls.

Sayaka, Haruka, and Koganemaru are also real potato varieties that happen to have names that sound like Japanese names.

Page 170
Ishigaki Island is a Japanese island west of Okinawa; the climate there is more tropical.

Page 185
The Kanto region is on Japan's main island, Honshu, and includes the Tokyo area and surrounding prefectures.

Silver Spoon

Silver Spoon 12

HIROMU ARAKAWA

Translation: Amanda Haley / **Lettering: Abigail Blackman**

GIN NO SAJI SILVER SPOON Vol. 12
by Hiromu ARAKAWA

Original Japanese edition published by SHOGAKUKAN.
English translation rights in the United States of America, Canada, the United Kingdom, Ireland, Australia and New Zealand arranged with SHOGAKUKAN through Tuttle-Mori Agency, Inc.

Yen Press
150 West 30th Street, 19th Floor
New York, NY 10001

Visit us at yenpress.com
facebook.com/yenpress
twitter.com/yenpress
yenpress.tumblr.com
instagram.com/yenpress

First Yen Press Edition: December 2019

Yen Press is an imprint of Yen Press, LLC.
The Yen Press name and logo are trademarks of Yen Press, LLC.

The publisher is not responsible for websites (or their content) that are not owned by the publisher.

Library of Congress Control Number: 2017959207

ISBN: 978-1-9753-5313-1

10 9 8 7 6 5 4 3 2

WOR

Printed in the United States of America